THE
IRANIAN
TIME
BOMB

THE IRANIAN TIME BOMB

The Mullah Zealots'
Quest for Destruction

MICHAEL A. LEDEEN

T·T

TRUMAN TALLEY BOOKS

ST. MARTIN'S PRESS ✻ NEW YORK

www.stmartins.com

Library of Congress Cataloging-in-Publication Data

Ledeen, Michael Arthur, 1941–
    The Iranian time bomb : the mullah zealots' quest for destruction / Michael A. Ledeen.
        p. cm.
    ISBN-13: 978-0-312-37655-0
    ISBN-10: 0-312-37655-3
    1. Iran—politics and government—1997– 2. United States—Foreign relations—Iran. 3. Iran—Foreign relations—United States. 4. Iran—Strategic aspects. 5. Terrorism—Religious aspects—Islam. I. Title.
    DS318.9.L43 2007
    955.05'44—dc22   2007018641

First Edition: September 2007

10 9 8 7 6 5 4 3 2 1

To Simone, Gabriel, and Daniel Ledeen.
They know, and they are fighting it.

CONTENTS

THE
IRANIAN
TIME
BOMB

INTRODUCTION

The Ayatollah Khomeini is "some kind of a saint."

—Andrew Young, American ambassador
to the United Nations, 1979

T*he Iranian Time Bomb* tells the story of the terror war waged against the Western world by the Islamic Republic of Iran, and the West's failure to respond effectively. Future historians will have to unravel the mystery of our remarkable refusal to fight back against an enemy that never hid its intention to destroy or dominate us, and impose a clerical fascism that is the antithesis of freedom.

Most people, even those who consider themselves well informed, do not realize that, for nearly thirty years, the Iranians continuously attacked us, and, aside from some harsh rhetoric from time to time, we never responded. President after president enabled the Iranians to buy modern weapons (sometimes selling them directly to the mullahs), and went to extraordinary lengths to try to work out a peaceful agreement with them. This was true regardless of political party, and regardless of the presidents' political ideology. It is true today. As I write, Secretary of State Condoleezza Rice is making an impassioned plea for Iranian leaders to join her in a conference in Egypt, and she is promising American concessions in exchange for small changes in the Iranian nuclear program.

This book documents the mystery, tries to explain it, and suggests it's time for us to fight back, using political and economic weapons, not military power. It begins with a description of the Revolution of 1979 that brought this regime to power, continues with a discussion of the nature of the regime, and then an analysis of the way the Islamic Republic is waging war against us. It then describes American policy toward Iran, and concludes with suggestions for a successful strategy.

Iranian behavior has not changed since the consolidation of Khomeini's power. The Shah was overthrown in the first months of 1979 by a revolutionary mass movement containing a cross section of the Iranian people, but while it took several years to totally eliminate the secular elements of the revolutionary coalition, the Iranian political system was transformed almost immediately into a theocratic state. The Islamic Republic of Iran was created by national referendum on March 30–31, 1979, barely a month after the fall of the Shah. The country's new leader, Ayatollah Ruhollah Khomeini, proclaimed the vote a religious act, declaring a vote against the Islamic Republic the equivalent of a vote against Islam itself. In like manner, anyone who protested against the wave of summary executions carried out by the new regime was held to be an enemy of the Islamic state, and Khomeini moved quickly to destroy the many European elements that the shah and his father had built into the Iranian judicial system. Henceforth, the strictest interpretations of Islamic (Sharia) law would govern the country; there could be no appeal from an Islamic judge's verdict, and every hearing required "a final absolute decision in a single phase."

Khomeini had long hated Western jurisprudence, as most everything at the heart of Judeo-Christian civilization. He had railed against the weakness of Western judges (and those Iranians who emulated them during the shah's time) for many decades, as we know from his sermons and pronouncements, many of which were collected and published in a 1975 book, *Khomeini and His Movement*. "In order to accomplish its own designs and to abolish manliness and adherence to Islam as qualities of judges," he intoned, "the government's Ministry of Justice has shown its opposition to the established laws of Islam. From this point on, Jews, Christians, and enemies of Islam and of the Muslims must not interfere in the affairs of Muslims."

This was certainly not an endorsement of an independent judiciary, since all meaningful power was concentrated in Khomeini's hands, and he was in a hurry to wipe out anything that smacked of what he constantly referred to as "satanic" Western influences.

The purge of Western legal principles and procedures went hand in hand with a rollback of most anything having to do with "modernity." Iranian women had gained ground under the two Pahlavi shahs, Reza and Mohammad Reza. Emulating Ataturk's reforms in Turkey, Reza Shah required men to wear Western clothes in all government offices, and taxes were eliminated on women's hats, stimulating Western headwear instead of scarves or chadors or hijabs. The veil was banned in 1936, and women started attending Tehran University at about the same time. In the 1960s, a Family Protection Law was passed, polygamy was limited, the marriage age raised, penalties on abortion eliminated, and women joined the electorate.

Khomeini rolled it all back. The Family Protection Law was undone, polygamy was reinstated, the hijab reinstituted, and all women eliminated from high official positions. They were encouraged to vote, a token concession undoubtedly granted with the dual aim of identifying malcontents and reassuring potentially hostile foreign powers. In any event, Iranian women weren't impressed:

the first open criticism of the Islamic Republic came from women, who protested the reactionary measures on March 8, 1979 (ever since, it has been celebrated as International Women's Day).

In September, a draft of the new constitution spelled out Khomeini's core vision of a theocratic state. The clerics would hold ultimate authority. And, crucially, "in the absence of the hidden Imam, guardianship of the affairs and leadership of the nation rests in the hands of the honest, efficient, and aware theologian whose leadership has been accepted and recognized by the majority of the people."

That "honest, efficient, and aware theologian" was Khomeini himself and represented a second revolution, this one within Shi'ism itself. Prior to 1979, Shi'ite wise men had always insisted that clerics should exercise moral and religious leadership—mostly in the mosques—and the affairs of civil society should be left in the hands of politicians. The reason for this was contained in the draft constitution, in words the faithful clearly understood: "in the absence of the hidden Imam . . ." So-called twelver Shi'ites (who constitute virtually all Iranian Muslims) believe that the fulfillment of Islam will only occur when the world is subjected to the rule of the twelfth legitimate ruler of the Muslim world (that is, the eleventh successor to the Prophet Muhammad). In their eyes, (illegitimate)

Sunni domination of the Muslim community was imposed by force in the ninth century, when, to save himself, the twelfth Imam—Muhammad al Mahdi—vanished in 874 at the age of seven. For some time, he managed to communicate with mankind, but he then entered the so-called Second Occultation, withdrawing entirely from the affairs of men. At some date in the future, the Mahdi will return and claim his rightful powers, but until then—according to traditional Shi'ite doctrine—it would be improper for any religious leader to claim secular power as well.

To be sure, the mullahs—the Shi'ite clerics—insisted that Sharia must be the law of the land, and many religious leaders exercised considerable power, but secular leaders were accepted as thoroughly legitimate, and the Shi'ite religious leaders claimed no special authority for themselves.

That long-standing doctrine was overturned by Khomeini, who produced the revolutionary concept of the *velayat i-faqih*, the rule of the supreme jurisprudent. With this doctrine, power would rest in Khomeini's hands, his legitimacy growing out of the consensus of the masses. Khomeini was proclaimed "Imam," thereby making him the country's Supreme Leader. This was theocracy, to be sure, but not of the sort envisaged by the Shi'ite sages. (Tellingly, when it came time to choose a successor, the constitution was changed, providing that future supreme leaders would be named by a council of religious experts. Khomeini was worried about competition from his peers; with the passage of time, the contempt of the people for the Islamic Republic became a more serious worry.)

Khomeini's theocratic dictatorship introduced a second radical element. Tradition required that his elevation as the leading ayatollah be sanctioned by others of his status. But Khomeini did not wish to rest his authority on the fickle alliances of his fellow clerics; instead, he stood upon the base of mass allegiance, which in 1979 and 1980 was beyond challenge. This was the Iranian version of the Hitlerian *Führerprinzip*, elaborated earlier in the century in the satanic West. Like the European fascists earlier in the century, Khomeini used the mass referendum as a means of consolidating his power.

Just as the European fascists aspired to global domination, Khomeini dreamed of extending the sway of his Islamic revolutionary doctrine all over the world. Khomeini believed he was leading a revolution that began in Iran and would spread throughout the Islamic world, then far beyond. Its domination of the Islamic world would be a vindication of Shi'ite doctrine at the expense of the Sunnis and would unleash a revolutionary jihad that would drive all vestiges of Western culture out of Muslim countries.

This global revolutionary vision has not changed in the twenty-eight years since the overthrow of the shah. Today, as during Khomeini's rule, the Supreme Leader views himself as the dominant figure in all of Islam. The Web site of the current "guide," Ali Khamenei, describes him as "the leader of the Muslims," endowed with the authority of the ancient Caliphs to lead all Muslims, not just the Iranian Shi'ites alone.

There were many such divisions (one of which was provoked by Khomeini's radical revision of Shi'ite doctrine regarding the role of clerics in the political sphere), of which the most famous was between Shi'ites and Sunnis. This originally stemmed from a dispute over the rightful successors to Muhammad, with each side accusing the other of illegitimacy. The Sunnis constitute about 80 percent of the Muslims.

Khamenei constantly warns against divisions within the ranks of the faithful. "Any divisive action in the Islamic world is a sin," he proclaimed at the beginning of the hajj in 2006. ". . . Those who insult the sanctities of various divisions of Islam . . . will be regarded as culprits, detested by history and future generations and looked upon as mercenaries of the brutal enemy."

It follows from this claim of universal validity—the core doctrine of the Khomeini Revolution—that the revolution must be exported by all ways and means, and calls for the export of the revolution were repeatedly heard from February 1979, on, from the Supreme Leader and his leading followers, directed variously against such moderate Middle Eastern countries as Egypt, Saudi Arabia, and Bahrain.

Moreover, one of Khomeini's most vicious cohorts, the Ayatollah Sadeq Khalkhali (best known for presiding over revolutionary tribunals that sent hundreds to their death in the immediate aftermath of the seizure of power), came up with a novel twist. He called for volunteers to travel overseas to assassinate family members and leaders of the shah's government, and he assured them their efforts would be protected. According to Khalkhali's creative reading of international law, even if the assassins were apprehended, they would be granted diplomatic immunity, since they would be recognized as representatives of the revolutionary government in Iran.

Khalkhali's view of assassination reflected the conviction that all Iranians were subject to the regime's desires. As with the other totalitarian regimes of the twentieth century, the Islamic Republic insisted that its citizens were liable for retribution no matter where they went. Internal repression went hand in hand with foreign assassinations, just as the Islamic Republic foreshadows what the mullahs plan is for the rest of the world.

The regime has used its iron fist both at home and

abroad. Those who protest have systematically been arrested, tortured, or executed. More than a hundred Iranians were assassinated in Europe, the United States, and the Middle East between 1979 and the beginning of 2001, in keeping with the straightforward pronouncement of Ahmad Janati, the secretary of the Council of Guardians, on June 15, 2001: "Those opposing the regime must be killed." Assassination is held in such high esteem that a street in central Tehran was renamed after Khaled Eslamboli, Anwar Sadat's killer. And the practice did not wane during the "reformist" years of President Mohammad Khatami, or the "pragmatic" years of President Hashemi Rafsanjani.

In keeping with his conviction that all Muslims should follow his example, Khomeini soon challenged the Sunnis' control over the holy sites of Mecca and Medina, even backing an armed protest during the hajj. And despite the centuries-old confrontation between Sunnis and Shi'ites, he unhesitatingly worked with Sunnis against their common enemies, a practice that began nearly a decade before the revolution, when Yasir Arafat's (Sunni) Fatah trained the precursors of the Iranian Revolutionary Guards in Lebanon. In public tribute to this invaluable assistance, Khomeini invited the PLO leader as the first foreign guest of the Islamic Republic and promised Arafat the PLO would receive a $1 royalty on every barrel of Iranian oil. It was a grand gesture, but only that; the Palestinians had to settle for the promise, as the money didn't arrive.

Khomeini's ambitions were not limited to the Middle East. From the moment of the overthrow of the shah, the leaders of the Islamic Republic have declared, and waged, war against the infidels of the West, above all against Americans and Israelis. The hostage crisis that doomed the Carter presidency was the opening salvo of a long war against America, branded the "Great Satan" by Khomeini. The principal instrument in this war has been the terrorist organization Hezbollah, which was created in Lebanon (where the Syrians provided safe haven in areas they occupied) shortly after the revolution. In the 1980s, Hezbollah—operating in tandem with the PLO—organized suicide bombing attacks against the French and American marine barracks, and the American embassy in Beirut, as well as the kidnappings of American missionaries and military and intelligence officers.

Two of the latter were then tortured to death. In the 1990s, Hezbollah conducted lethal attacks against Jewish targets in Argentina, for which leaders of the Iranian regime have been indicted.

Throughout this period, and contrary to a long-standing myth—according to which Sunnis and Shi'ites hate one another so much they cannot cooperate, even against a common enemy—Iran worked closely with

Sunni terrorists, just as the Revolutionary Guards and Arafat's Fatah worked to prepare the Iranian Revolution. The most dramatic example is its close relationship with Osama bin Laden's Al Qaeda. The 1998 embassy bombings in East Africa—for which Al Qaeda took full credit—were in large part Iranian operations. Bin Laden had asked Hezbollah's operational chieftain, Imad Mughniyah, for help making Al Qaeda as potent as Hezbollah, and the original concept for the simultaneous bombings in Kenya and Tanzania came directly from Mughniyah. The Al Qaeda terrorists were trained by Hezbollah in Lebanon, and the explosives were provided by Iran. After the attacks, one of the leaders of the operations, Saif al-Adel, took refuge in Iran, where he remains active today.

Despite all this evidence, it became a near unassailable conviction that Sunnis and Shi'ites just could not work together. It remains a recurring theme among academics and government experts and is the conventional wisdom in the intelligence community and at Foggy Bottom. But nobody told the Iranians or their Sunni allies.

The myth of an all-but-unbridgeable chasm between the Sunnis and Shi'ites underlies the failure of the American intelligence community to recognize that Iran aided both Sunni and Shi'ite terrorists in Iraq against Americans and Iraqis—and against each other—following the defenestration of Saddam Hussein in 2003. Indeed, Iran attempted to foment civil war all over Iraq, aiding both sides in every potential conflict, from Sunni vs. Shi'ite to Turkomans vs. Kurds, Arabs vs. Kurds, and so on. It was simply a continuation of the mullahs' war against America, which had been under way for nearly three decades.

Not that the Iranians preferred joint operations with the Sunnis to Shi'ite ones, of which there were many (mostly involving Hezbollah). An American federal judge, Royce Lamberth, recently ruled that Iran was responsible for the 1996 Khobar Towers bombing in Saudi Arabia, in which nineteen American air force personnel were killed and 372 wounded. The ruling was based in large part on sworn testimony from former FBI director Louis Freeh, who had investigated the bombings at the time they took place. Freeh found that two Iranian government security agencies and senior members of the Iranian government (including Supreme Leader Khamenei and intelligence chief Ali Fallahian) provided funding, training, explosives, and logistical assistance to the terrorists (who referred to themselves as "Saudi Hezbollah," thereby explicitly confirming their ties to the mullahs).

This was only the latest in a long series of public revelations about Iran's role in the Khobar Towers massacre and other terrorist attacks against America by top officials of the U.S. government. In the autumn of 1999, State Department spokesman James Rubin confirmed,

"We do have specific information with respect to the involvement of Iranian government officials [in the Khobar Towers bombing]." An indictment filed by the Justice Department in 2001 alleged Iranian direction of, and logistical support for, the attack—and noted that arrested conspirators confessed that the purpose of the attack was to strike the United States on behalf of Iran. Barely a week before the judicial finding, State Department counselor Philip Zelikow said, "During the 1990s, Iran aided terrorist groups that were targeting Americans, Israelis, and Saudis. Agents of the Iranian government were involved in the attack on the U.S. air force barracks at Khobar Towers, in Saudi Arabia, in 1996."

It is often said that our invasion of Iraq opened the door to an expansion of Iranian power in the Middle East. No doubt there is an element of truth in this claim, but it is an odd way of saying that Iran was determined to drive us out of Iraq and Afghanistan and used the same methods—suicide terrorism, kidnapping, mass indoctrination, and a combination of assistance to the poor with recruitment among them—that they had successfully employed in Lebanon a generation earlier. It took the American government more than three years before it realized that Iran was the engine within much of the "insurgency" in Iraq, as within the Taliban in Afghanistan. This latest intelligence failure proved fatal to a considerable number of Americans, Iraqis, British, Italian, Spanish, Polish, and other members of the coalition, along with many more Iraqis, in and out of uniform.

This is only one of many American failures to understand the nature of the Iranian jihad.

Even the dean of geopolitics balks at accepting the true nature of the Islamic Republic. Just before Thanksgiving 2006, Henry Kissinger addressed the Iran question in the traditional language of realpolitik. He treated Iran as a nation seeking geopolitical advantage, and he dealt with the nuclear question in that context: "Iran's nuclear program and considerable resources enable it to strive for strategic dominance in its region."[1]

Then, in a single sentence, he leaped to a global framework, in which ideology overwhelms national considerations: "With the impetus of a radical Shia ideology and the symbolism of defiance of the UN Security Council's resolution, Iran challenges the established order in the Middle East and perhaps wherever Islamic populations face dominant, non-Islamic majorities."

That is indeed the proper context. The mullahs see themselves as revolutionary figures who will transform the entire world. Iran's Supreme Leader, whether

---

[1] Henry Kissinger, "What Do We Do with Iran?" *Khaleej Times*, November 17, 2006.

Khomeini or Khamenei, claims to be the sole legitimate guide for all Muslims. He speaks in the name of a Shi'ite revolution that far transcends mere national ambition. If you want to understand what radical Islam is all about, you can't do better than memorize the words of the Ayatollah Khomeini at the time of the hostage crisis, way back in 1979: "We do not worship Iran. We worship Allah. For patriotism is another name for paganism. I say let this land [Iran] burn. I say let this land go up in smoke, provided Islam emerges triumphant in the rest of the world."

Kissinger finesses this central fact, which lies at the core of the Iranian Revolution. After tiptoing up to it, he slides back into the traditional language, as if Khomeinist Iran were a traditional nation-state. The rest of the essay mostly addresses the nuclear question alone, and how "diplomacy" can and should deal with it. It's a peculiar discussion, based on at least one totally unknowable assumption. "Teheran sees no compelling national interest to give up its claim to being a nuclear power," he says quite rightly, but then launches into the unknown, "and strong domestic political reasons to persist. Pursuing the nuclear weapons program is a way of appealing to national pride and shores up an otherwise shaky domestic support."

Lots of people say that sort of thing—that the Iranian

people really want their government to have nuclear weapons—but there is no reliable polling data to support it, and the anecdotal "evidence" is all over the lot.

I think we should take the leaders of the Islamic Republic at their word. They say they do not think of themselves as national leaders, and they openly despise patriotism; "another name for paganism" does not bespeak national pride. At one point Kissinger suggests that Western "diplomacy" must be aimed at convincing the Iranian leaders that they should think of their country in traditional terms, and not as "a crusade." But they don't. Without exception, their core beliefs are totally contrary to the notion they are a traditional nation-state. To ask them to think in this way is like trying to use negotiations to convince the pope that he should think of himself as the grand duke of Vatican City rather than the vicar of Christ on earth.

Kissinger's refusal to acknowledge the religious and revolutionary nature of the Islamic Republic is of a piece with the refrain from scores of American and European diplomats who insist that negotiations can eventually tame the Islamic Revolution. It won't work. Only the defeat of the Islamic Republic can accomplish that goal, because that would demonstrate that the mullahs do not have divine support for their global jihad.

There's something about diplomats, no matter how

brilliant, that leads them into a world that never existed and most likely never will. The results achieved by the grand master of diplomacy were, after all, often disappointing. Kissinger attempted to tame the Soviet empire by constructing "détente," which probably extended the life of the communist superstate by a decade or more; it took Ronald Reagan to bring it to a close. Kissinger attempted to negotiate peace between Israel and its enemies, thereby spinning out a grand illusion—the misnamed "peace process"—that has created a cottage industry for negotiators but an expanded war for the citizens of the region. The illusion that "diplomacy" can accomplish anything worthwhile with the Islamic Republic of Iran will only intensify the mullahs' conviction that killing Americans is divinely sanctioned and a winning strategy.

This dangerous mind-set has seized the minds of American diplomats from the first days of the Iranian Revolution. It was elegantly described by Matthias Küntzel, reflecting on the shock experienced by Bruce Laingen, the number two diplomat in the American embassy in Tehran, when he was taken hostage by the Iranians in 1979:

Bruce Bowden invokes the shock that the first encounter with real Islamism represented [to our diplomats]. He describes how "the entire professional frame of reference" of embassy chargé d'affaires Bruce E. Laingen had to be overturned. Before the hostage-taking, Laingen possessed, in Bowden's expression, "a constitutional bias toward hope." He strongly believed that "things were getting better [in Iran]" and put all his trust in "the power of polite dialogue between nations." Laingen was, in Bowden's words, "bewildered" by the events of November 4. "Why? To what end?" he wrote in his journal four days after the seizure of the embassy.

It is eery to watch Condoleezza Rice and her European peers evince the same frame of mind today, twenty-eight years later. No matter how much evidence of Iran's determination to destroy or dominate us, no matter how many times Khamenei or Ahmadinejad lead the chant of "Death to America" or "Death to the infidels," she and the other wishful diplomats of this world continue to convince themselves that the Iranian leaders share our goals for peace (or, to use one of their favorite words, "stability") in the region, and that if we only make one more generous offer or hold one more private schmooze, the whole unpleasant situation will work out for the best.

It is not so, and our most honest diplomats know it. In fact, we have been negotiating with the mullahs ever since—indeed even before—the 1979 revolution. The lack of any tangible result is obvious, yet the advocates of negotiation act as if none of this ever happened.

Many will be surprised to discover that every American administration since the Islamic Revolution, from Jimmy Carter's to George W. Bush's, has believed it possible to strike a grand bargain with the mullahs. Only once—during Reagan's tenure—did American forces seriously engage those of the Islamic Republic, and that was in response to an Iranian assault on American navy vessels in the Gulf. Not once has any American president approved a policy of supporting a change in the Tehran regime.

In pursuit of this bargain, we've distorted many elements of traditional American foreign policy. We have refrained from openly supporting the tens of millions of Iranian dissidents who periodically show their contempt for the regime by demonstrating, going on strike, or fighting back against their oppressors. Indeed, in an effort to demonstrate our "goodwill" to the mullahs, we have frequently violated our own policies, especially when it came to arms sales or transfers. The Carter administration offered to arm the revolutionary regime within days of the fall of the shah; the Reagan administration secretly sold weapons to Tehran and provided the mullahs with military intelligence to help in their war against Saddam Hussein's Iraq; the Clinton administration secretly permitted the

Iranians to arm Bosnian Muslim fighters in the Balkans and secretly permitted the Russians to arm the Iranians and support their nuclear program.

Clinton showered largesse on the Iranians and even dispatched his secretary of state to apologize for real and imagined American sins in decades past. Encouraged by the election of a "reformist" Iranian president, Mohammad Khatami, we opened a channel of communications to the highest levels of the regime, liberalized our visa policies, expanded cultural exchanges, and removed the Islamic Republic from the State Department's lists of state sponsors of terrorism and narcotrafficking governments. We even eased the trade embargo. Then came Secretary of State Madeleine Albright's open apology. She apologized for the American role in restoring the shah to his throne in the 1950s. She apologized for American support to the Shah prior to the revolution, and for "regrettably shortsighted" help given to Iraq during the war.

Clinton's many gestures, concessions, and giveaways, like those of his predecessors, produced a swift kick to a delicate part of our national anatomy. Supreme Leader Ali Khamenei summarily rejected the American démarche and reiterated the Islamic Republic's passionate hatred for the American "Great Satan."

Even the Bush administration, which famously placed

Iran alongside North Korea and Iraq as a charter member of the "Axis of Evil," pursued a grand bargain with the mullahs, and American officials sometimes made statements—as when Deputy Secretary of State Richard Armitage proclaimed that the Islamic Republic was a democracy—that can only be explained as an effort to woo the Iranian leaders. And the Bush team, like those that came before it, rarely paid the slightest attention to the extraordinary cruelty with which the mullahs have repressed the Iranian people. Instead of speaking out on behalf of the brave Iranians who call for freedom, we have courted their torturers. In early 2003, Michael Rubin wrote about the treatment of Siamak Pourzand, an elderly journalist who was arrested when he advocated democracy. Locked in solitary confinement and brutally tortured, he was forced to make a televised confession of crimes he had not committed. Broken by his torturers, Pourzand suffered a heart attack and fell into a coma.

> He is chained to a bed in Tehran's Modarres Hospital. His weight has dropped to fifty-five kilograms. The Islamic Republic continues to deprive him of essential medical care. As much as European Union officials and Armitage speak of progress and reform in Iran, democracies do not torture seventy-five-year-old men. If Pourzand awakes from his coma, he will not see U.S.

diplomats holding Tehran accountable for his health and well-being. Rather, Pourzand will see Iranian news reports of former and current members of the U.S. National Security Council greeting figures like Mohsen Rezai, a former commander of the Islamic Revolutionary Guard Corps.[2]

Those who still dream of the grand bargain—including those in the G. W. Bush administration who have pursued it avidly and have repeatedly gotten kicked in the same delicate part of the anatomy as the impassioned suitors of the Clinton years—cannot explain why there is anything different today that might make a bargain with the Iranians more likely than it has been for twenty-eight years. Certainly the Iranians have shown no desire for reconciliation; quite the contrary, unless you think killing Americans on a scale considerably larger than the tempo of murder in the Clinton years represents some odd form of mating dance. The Supreme Leader is the same fanatic as then, to be sure in terrible health, but not noticeably friendlier toward satanic Americans. The only big change in Tehran personnel is the president. Instead of Khatami the Reformer we've got Ahmadinejad,

---

[2] Michael Rubin, "Half-Hearted: Bold words but weak action from the Bush administration," *National Review Online*, April 26, 2004.

Hitler's great admirer. That is certainly not an improvement; if anything, it would seem to make the argument for negotiations weaker than at any time since the Revolution.

The mullahs do not share our dreams; they dream of our destruction. Early in 2007, the official Web site of the Iranian broadcasting system posted an essay entitled "The World Toward Illumination."[3] It begins with a denunciation of the Western world and a forecast of its imminent demise: "Lack of attention to man's sublime needs in these societies has created social and cultural crises. Thus this civilization like those of many of Western theoreticians is just an unreal theory. It seems that in the same way that . . . Imam Khomeini predicted the fall of communism we must get ready to search for the liberal democratic civilization in history museums."

Western civilization will be consigned to the garbage heap of history by the twelfth Imam. "When he reappears, peace, justice, and security will overcome oppression and deceit, and one global government, the most perfect ever, will be established."

These are dreams of global conquest and domination,

---

[3] Memri, "Waiting for the Mahdi: Official Iranian Eschatology Outlined in Public Broadcasting Program in Iran," Memri Special Dispatch Series no. 1436, January 25, 2007.

and they think they are winning. The terror war against us now extends to four continents, running from Thailand and Indonesia to India and Pakistan, down the Horn of Africa to Somalia and Yemen and back up to Afghanistan, on to Iraq, Palestine/Israel, and Lebanon, and thence to Europe, the United States, and South America. The Iranians are involved in every one of those theaters and they believe they are making good progress everywhere. They think they have defeated us in Iraq, and that we will soon leave, humiliated by their superior resolve and broken by the willing sacrifice of thousands of martyrs. They believe they defeated Israel in the summer war of 2006, that they will expand their control over Lebanon in the near future and in relatively short order destroy the Jewish state. They fully expect to compel us to surrender and submit to their will.

Diplomacy will not tame them. We can win or lose, but we cannot escape this confrontation. As Salim Mansur puts it, "To achieve peace and freedom the most bigoted elements within the Muslim world—the jihadi Muslims and their allies—need to be irrevocably defeated."

Iran is the most powerful element among the jihadi Muslims, and, as Mansur continues, "they will continue to seek to take advantage of the cracks and divisions among non-Muslims to consolidate their own power. They will wage their war in as many ways as they can, openly and by deceit, and ruthlessly repress any dissent among Muslims and non-Muslims wherever they prevail. This the world must realize."[4]

When the great scholar Bernard Lewis presented an analysis of the state of affairs in Washington in early March 2007, he noted that the Islamic fascists had many advantages over the West. They were totally committed to their mission, while the West was divided and uncertain. They believed in the superiority of their beliefs, while the West was often paralyzed by doubt and the moral equivalence that goes under the name of multiculturalism. They embraced death, while the West mourned every human loss. But the West, he said, also had advantages, both material and moral, of which the greatest was the idea of freedom. This idea, which is the basis for our society and the highest good in our political vision, has only recently begun to penetrate the Islamic world, but it has the potential to ruin all their dreams of triumphant jihad. It is our greatest weapon in the war, and that is nowhere so dramatically evident as in Iran.

The Islamic Republic of Iran is a monumental failure by any civilized measure. Students of revolutions will easily identify the many aspects of contemporary Iran

---

[4] Salim Mansur, "The Cool Water of the Koran (Part III)," www.pajamasmedia.com, March 3, 2007.

that make it vulnerable to a popular uprising: a failed economy; visible degradation of cities and infrastructure; virtual epidemics of drug abuse, sex trafficking, and prostitution; a young, volatile population that openly challenges the regime and indeed Islam itself; the manifest bankruptcy of a regime that does not pay teachers or workers for months on end; the widespread indifference to the doctrines of the Shi'ite faith. With more than 65 percent of the young population (two-thirds of Iranians are under thirty years of age) below the poverty line in 2005, it is no wonder that there are demonstrations against the widely detested regime all over the country. Nor is it surprising that some of the oppressed ethnic and religious minorities have launched armed attacks against the Revolutionary Guards Corps and the fanatical Basij forces, the prime instruments of oppression. There are open denunciations of President Ahmadinejad, of former President Rafsanjani, and even of Supreme Leader Khamenei. All this is taking place against the background of a cancer-ridden Supreme Leader who is expected to die in the near future, and an intense struggle for succession.

After twenty-eight years of Iranian war waged against us, we are slowly beginning to respond. Late last autumn, our troops in Iraq were authorized to shoot or arrest Iranians believed to be involved in training, paying, or arming terrorists. And for the first time since the beginning of Operation Iraqi Freedom, captured Iranians have been kept in jail rather than sent back across the border.

It is a good start, but only that. Sooner or later we will have to contend with the Tehran regime itself. The slow fuse of the Iranian time bomb was lit in 1979 and is now burning down toward nuclear weapons. If we do not extinguish it, we risk the terrible consequences of its explosion.

1 THE TORTURE MASTERS

At the very least, you could have given me a glass of water. Animals are slaughtered more humanely than this.

> —Atefeh Rajabi, sixteen years of age, about
> to be hanged for "adultery," August 15, 2004

Absolutely, we do have political prisoners. There are those who are in prison for their beliefs.

> —"Reformist" president Mohammad
> Khatami, April 28, 2004

In the months following his successful revolution against the shah, the Ayatollah Khomeini consolidated his domestic power through the use of four basic techniques:

- The first, common to all modern fascist movements, was the constant mobilization of the masses. The mobilization exploited the symbols and doctrines of Islamic fundamentalism, and the techniques of twentieth-century mass movements, from monster rallies, constant incitement to hatred of the revolution's "satanic" enemies (of which the United States and Israel were the prime examplars), and, once Saddam attacked and the bloody Iran-Iraq war began, constant reference to martyrdom. A fountain in downtown Tehran was stocked with red liquid, to represent the blood of the martyrs.

• Second, the regime devoted constant attention to the needs of the most impoverished sectors of the society. In a sort of Shi'ite version of Robin Hood, money, food, and housing were seized from the old elites and redistributed to the very poor. Khomeini even exempted the poor from paying taxes, and they were provided with free transportation. The regime's largesse was extended to workers as well, especially those in the oil fields, whose salaries were quickly and dramatically increased. This ensured the loyalty of the lower classes and kept the well-to-do constantly concerned about their own well-being.

• Third was total, uncompromising war against anything having to do with the West. As the Taliban would famously do in Afghanistan after the defeat of the Red Army, Khomeini banned music. Western books were removed from the schools and often burned. Above all, a strict segregation of the sexes was imposed throughout the educational system. Women would no longer be permitted to teach boys, and women were subjected to the humiliations described earlier: polygamy was reinstituted (with the additional fillip that "temporary marriages"—perhaps long enough for an afternoon tryst—were legalized, in order to finesse charges of adultery), along with the veil, and divorce initiated by women was made far more difficult.

• Fourth was the use of the judicial system as an instrument of terror. As so often happens at moments of dramatic change, the institution was marked by the ghoulish personality of its first leader, the Ayatollah Khalkhali. He had two nicknames, the Butcher of Kurdistan, and the Cat Killer. The first was earned in a murderous campaign against the Kurds in mid-1979. Khalkhali had hundreds of them lined up and executed by firing squads en masse. The second derived from rumors that the man was literally mad and relieved his mental torment by strangling and dismembering cats. He treated his human victims with the same compulsive violence; a year and a half after the seizure of power, he told an interviewer that he had probably ordered the execution of four or five hundred "sinners."[1] In the first seven months of Khomeini's rule, the revolutionary tribunals killed off more than six hundred people, including many who had wielded great power under the old regime.

This method of seizing and maintaining power has subsequently been used as a template for the export of the revolution. The mullahs have attempted to export the revolution to many countries, from Saudi Arabia to Bosnia, each time using a mixture of religious proselytizing and terror. By and large, these efforts have failed, but the one great foreign success of the Islamic Republic[2]—the creation of Hezbollah in Lebanon—clearly follows the revolutionary model. Hezbollah is at once a political party, a philanthropic organization that pays particular attention to the poor, and the world's most lethal terrorist organization. In its domain in southern Lebanon, the

---

[1] In *l'Express* (Paris), June 21, 1980. Some excerpts in English are in Michael Ledeen, "Presswatch," *American Spectator*, August 1980.
[2] The other considerable Iranian success is Bosnia, which is discussed in greater detail in chapter 3.

"party of Allah" enforces the rules of a Khomeini-style theocratic state and enthusiastically spreads the faith by preaching, paying, and bullying the populace. These practices are well-known in Lebanon, and they are spreading. Iran's strategic Siamese twin, Syria, recently approved Shi'ite proselytizing, and the Iranians quickly sent mullahs to preach the virtues of Khomeinism, sweetening the prospects of eternal salvation with cash grants of $10,000 per convert.

Hezbollah's political strength in Lebanon rests on the many acts of charity and public works performed in its stronghold: housing construction, education, health care, and charity. That system is brilliantly conceived to achieve a double objective, just as Khomeini's was. At the same time it delivers much needed assistance to the needy, it creates a mass base of true believers who then assist in recruiting terrorists for both domestic and foreign operations, while concealing the clandestine activities of the armed party. Its efficacy in Lebanon was demonstrated in the summer war of 2006, when Israel—whose ability to gather intelligence on its enemies is legendary—was amazed at Hezbollah's discipline, logistics, military technology, and imaginative tactics. All had effectively been concealed from Israeli military intelligence and Mossad.

When the Israelis sat down after the war to analyze

the "lessons learned," they realized that Hezbollah and Iran had created a model for consolidating power, then striven to apply it all over the Islamic world. Once they looked at Iran in that way, the Israelis saw that the Hezbollah model was being installed on their own border: "The Iranians have been working to create a model in Gaza via Hamas that is similar to Hezbullah's southern Lebanon model . . . the same system that supports civil affairs . . . also creates a civilian infrastructure for terror."[3] That terror is aimed against both internal and external enemies.

Modern tyrannies have invariably dehumanized entire classes or races, to impose their will on the pure and faithful and rally them to wage war against their foes. This is not a random process; Nazi dehumanization of the Jews, Communist dehumanization of the capitalist bourgeoisie, and the Islamist dehumanization of the "crusaders and infidels" are totally at peace with their official worldview. As Natan Sharansky reminds us, the regimes that support terror against foreign foes also direct terror at their own people, and thus it is no accident that Iran is at once the world's leading supporter of international terrorism and one of the cruelest oppressors of its own people.

---

[3] *Iran, Hizbullah, Hamas and the Global Jihad: A New Conflict Paradigm for the West* (Jerusalem: Jerusalem Center for Public Affairs, 2007).

In the Iranian case, the external enemies are primarily the Jews, Zionists, and Americans, the lesser and greater Satans against whom the divinely inspired Islamic Revolution constantly fights. The internal enemies comprise anyone who challenges the wisdom or legitimacy of the regime . . . and women, who are viewed as the ultimate source of corruption. Khomeini was a supreme misogynist, and the laws of the Islamic Republic single out women for special horrors and humiliation.

WOMEN

The oppression and even torture of Iranian women was an integral part of the Islamic Revolution and is embodied in the strictures of Khomeini's constitution for the Islamic Republic. A woman's worth is officially defined as half of a man's. Iranian law provides for the payment of "blood money" in the case of violent crime or accident, and harm to a man costs twice as much as the same damage to a woman. A man killed in an automobile incident gets twice as much as a woman killed in the same event. Incredibly, if a pregnant woman is killed, the guilty party pays the full assessment for the dead male fetus but only half as much for its mother.

Women are systematically dominated by men in every

aspect of civil life. No Iranian woman, no matter how old or distinguished, can marry without her father's or paternal grandfather's consent, or if that cannot be obtained, the approval of a religious tribunal. Mothers don't count. Indeed, although a woman is only recognized as a citizen once she is a mother (and therefore has no legal standing so long as she is single), mothers have no say in the marriage of their children. It is all in the hands of the men.

Given this absolute authority, in many cases young girls (the legal age for marriage is thirteen) are married off to older, even elderly men, because of financial advantage. This sort of treatment also takes place at the opposite end of the age line: girls are instructed to marry young boys (who are eligible at fifteen). Unsurprisingly, a high percentage of divorces involve partners who married when they were under nineteen years of age.

Men can divorce their wives whenever they wish, but women must prove that the husband has misbehaved, which includes drug addiction, conviction for crimes, or failure to provide for the wife's subsistence. Since the men are invariably favored by the courts, women often find it impossible to get a divorce without the husband's cooperation, and this generally requires them to formally renounce their legal right to financial support. In Qom, for example, a recent study found that more than 90 percent of divorced women had either abandoned all claim to support or had negotiated a reduction.

Almost all of the tiny handful of Iranian women in positions of authority (only 4 percent of the members of the recently elected parliament are female, and not one was a candidate for a leadership position) endorse the subordination of women.[4] One such parliamentarian, Nayereh Akhavaran, remarked, in fine Khomeini-style rhetoric, "Man's right to divorce comes from the fact that because women are emotional, they may destroy everything. But with the right to divorce in man's hands, they will stop the destruction of the family."

The same prejudicial treatment applies to guardianship of children. Iranian civil law denies women the right to legal guardianship; the father always rules supreme, and he cannot ever delegate parental authority to his wife. If he dies, control passes to his own father. And if both are absent or dead, the child then becomes a ward of the state, never of the mother. Mothers, even married mothers, cannot do any of the routine things they do in the West: they can't open a bank account in their children's name, can't approve medical treatment, can't even buy a house for their children. Indeed, even if a house is

---

[4] Mercedes Khagani, "Who Supports the Violation of Women's Rights?" *Roozonline*, February 6, 2007.

purchased with the father's full approval, the mother has no rights with regard to it, while the father can do whatever he wants.

Women have no right to own property, and a wife only receives a fraction of her husband's estate when she is widowed, and of course sons receive twice as much as daughters. If there was more than one wife, the same fraction of the estate—one-eighth or one-fourth, depending on whether there were children—is divided among the widows. As usual, if the situation is reversed, and the wife dies first, the widower gets double: one-fourth or one-half of the estate.

The most humiliating case is if there are no children and the husband dies. The widow gets the usual one-fourth of the estate, and the rest goes to the Islamic Republic. As a leading Iranian feminist puts it, "The government is closer to that man than his wife with whom he has lived an entire lifetime."

Everything is patrilineal, even citizenship. If an Iranian woman marries a foreigner, the children are not considered to be Iranian, unless the mother has received special approval from the Interior Ministry, and she may even lose her own citizenship.

Polygamy is fine for men (up to four "permanent" wives are permitted, plus a limitless number of "temporary" partners) but denied to women (and the chair of the

Parliamentary Women's Faction endorses polygamy: "This is eventually in the interest of women, and women should accept it"). Consequently, men rarely if ever stand trial for adultery, while female adulterers are subject to the barbaric practice of stoning to death. Not surprisingly, most of the cases of women murdering their husbands stem from the man's infidelity, whatever the largesse of the "temporary marriage" proviso. Here again, the double standard is in full force. Women who murder their unfaithful husband are punished, while a man will go scot-free if he kills his wife if he discovers—or even imagines—that she has been intimate with other men.

Finally, just as the Jews were once forced to wear distinctive clothing, so Iranian women must wear the hijab. This applies to all women, whatever their religion. Muslims, Baha'is, Christians, and Jews all must dress in the same way.

No surprise, then, that laws have been drafted to reduce the number of women admitted to university study, and to forbid travel outside the Islamic Republic for single women. No surprise, either, that Iranian activists are quietly circulating a petition calling for equal rights for women. Their objective is to gather a million signatures and then submit it to the parliament. The regime dreads this—it is hardly a secret, having appeared on many blogs and been announced in public meetings in the major cities—and anyone caught soliciting signatures goes straight to jail.

The brutal treatment of Iranian women by the mullahcracy occurs daily, not in isolated cases. As *Iran Focus* reported on March 2, 2005, "At least fifty-four Iranian girls and young women, between the ages of sixteen and twenty-five, are sold on the streets of Karachi in Pakistan on a daily basis," according to "a senior women's affairs analyst . . . speaking to a state-run news agency." The analyst, Mahboubeh Moghadam, added that there are at least three hundred thousand runaway girls in Iran right now, the result, in Moghadam's words, of "the government policy which has resulted in poverty and the deprival of rights for the majority of people in society."

Moghadam suggested (and remember that this did not come from a samizdat network, but from a broadcast on Iranian national radio) "that such a task was very difficult to carry out without some sort of government green light."

Professor Donna M. Hughes, at the University of Rhode Island, one of the few Western scholars reporting on these horrors, says that the enslaved women are typically sold to people in the Arab countries of the Persian Gulf, such as Qatar, Kuwait, and the United Arab Emirates. But the slave trade is not limited to the Islamic world.

Police have uncovered a number of prostitution and

slavery rings operating from Tehran that have sold girls to France, Britain, and Turkey as well. One network based in Turkey bought smuggled Iranian women and girls, gave them fake passports, and transported them to European and Persian Gulf countries. In one case, a sixteen-year-old girl was smuggled to Turkey, then sold to a fifty-eight-year-old European national for $20,000.

There are countless examples of the maltreatment of Iranian women, but none so dramatic as the case of a foreigner of Iranian origin who tried to expose the regime's systematic oppression of those seeking greater freedom for all Iranians.

In the summer of 2003, a middle-aged Iranian-Canadian journalist named Zahra Kazemi was arrested in Tehran while taking photographs of regime hoodlums beating up young people demonstrating against the regime. A few days later she turned up dead in a local military hospital. The regime denied requests from the family and the Canadian government to examine the body, insisted that she had fallen in her prison cell and died of head injuries resulting from the fall, denied that anyone had beaten her, and hastily buried her without any proper autopsy.

The Kazemi family never believed the regime's story, but efforts to get at the truth were predictably fruitless. It was one of those things that "everybody knew," but it could not be documented sufficiently to convince the skeptics and apologists for the mullahs. Then, in the spring of 2005, a medical doctor named Shahram Azam was granted asylum in Canada and presented a firsthand account of the terrible death of Zahra Kazemi.[5]

Dr. Azam said he examined Kazemi in a military hospital in Tehran on June 26, 2003. He said he found horrific injuries to her entire body that demonstrated torture and a nurse's examination suggested rape. By the time he examined her—an examination limited by the Islamic Republic's sexist restrictions that made it illegal for a male doctor to look at her genital area—Kazemi was unconscious and her body was covered with bruises. According to Dr. Azam, she had a skull fracture, two broken fingers, missing fingernails, a crushed big toe, a smashed nose, deep scratches on her neck, and evidence of flogging on her legs and back.

"I could see this was caused by torture," Azam told Canadian journalists. He added that the nurse who examined Kazemi's genitals told him of "brutal damage," which led him to conclude she was raped.

All of this is consistent with what we have learned

---

[5] This analysis first appeared in Michael Ledeen, "Save the Women, Save Ourselves," *National Review Online*, April 4, 2005.

about the methods of torture routinely employed in Iranian prisons and reported by leading international human rights organizations from Human Rights Watch and Amnesty International to Reporters Without Borders and the State Department's survey of human rights around the world. These sadistic practices are directed against all critics and opponents of the regime, but they are carried out with particular energy when the victim is female, a legacy from the founder. Misogyny was famously one of Khomeini's personal obsessions.

POLITICAL DISSIDENTS

The cheerless creatures who rule the Islamic Republic of Iran have developed a particularly wicked use of torture. Not only do they use the full panoply of physical and psychological horrors on their captives, but they then send the victims back into their homes and neighborhoods for brief periods of "parole" or "medical leave," so that their friends and families can see with their own eyes the brutal effects of the torture. This is certainly not an expression of tenderness toward the mullahs' targets, but a demonstration that the regime has understood that torture is far more effective on the population at large when its effects are there for everyone to see. The clear intent of this unusual practice is to intimidate the population at large, to break the will of would-be dissenters and opponents, and to maximize the effects on the victims themselves, for the brief respite from the pain of the prisons is mercilessly accompanied by the certainty that the agony will soon resume. That knowledge makes it more likely that the prisoners will break and cooperate with the regime. The mullahs love show trials and are willing to be generous to dissidents who abandon their opposition and cooperate with the system. The Soviets would extort false confessions and then kill their victims; the mullahs are more refined. They are quite willing to kill their challengers, but they calculate that it is often more valuable to leave the "guilty" at large—carrying the physical and emotional scars of their brutal treatment—as proof that opposition to the regime is hopeless.

Thus, when a victim uses his time outside the torture chambers to call for the people of Iran to act against the regime, it warrants our attention. If the Western political leaders were willing to openly challenge the mullahs, or if the organizations who champion "human rights" were more aggressive in fulfilling their own mission statements, we would know the names of these brave Iranians, and we would give them, and the Iranian people more broadly, the kind of support they deserve.

GANJI

One of the most prominent dissenters, a distinguished journalist named Akbar Ganji, was given a weeklong "medical leave" from Evin Prison in Tehran in June 2005 and promptly gave an Internet interview that nearly proved fatal. He called for a general boycott of the "make-believe elections" for the presidency, scheduled for the seventeenth of the month, and urged the Iranian people to engage in large-scale civil disobedience.

"We are faced with a personal dictatorship, the dictatorship of [Supreme Leader Ali] Khamenei," he said. "Khamenei has ruled for fifteen years and wants to rule for life. I oppose this and I say that this contradicts democracy." Ganji called for Khamenei himself to submit his dictatorial rule to a public ratification. "He must take part in a free election; should the people vote him in, he can rule, and should they reject him, he must step aside."[6]

Paradoxically, this was the way Khomeini had consolidated his own power. Instead of seeking election from his peers, the old ayatollah had organized a national referendum. But Ganji was right; by the time he gave his interview,

---

[6] Quoted in Michael Ledeen, "The War Against the Torture Masters," *National Review Online*, June 8, 2005.

the great majority of Iranians had soured on the Islamic Republic, and it was highly unlikely that the Supreme Leader would be confirmed in a free and fair election. And Ganji's provocation, a direct challenge to the legitimacy of the Islamic Republic, was met with the regime's usual brutality. Following the interview, the head of the Evin Prison announced that Akbar Ganji had to return at once. He proved an extremely able challenger; once in jail he went on a hunger strike that reportedly savaged his health to the point that he went into a coma. President Bush called for his release. International organizations echoed the call. Under all this pressure, the mullahs relented, taking him from prison to a hospital, where he was rehydrated and, after some delay, delivered to his family.

Perhaps the regime knew by then that they had accomplished at least part of their goal, for the Ganji who had been brought back from the edge of death was no longer the forceful campaigner who had demanded that the regime submit to the people's will; he continued to speak for greater freedom in Iran, but much more quietly, and he no longer insisted on a prompt election for the Islamic Republic's top position. Indeed, the regime sent him on a Western tour, where he spent most of his time denouncing American pressure on the mullahs.

The Iranian torturers do their work well; Ganji is not the first dissident to decide not to sacrifice his own life, or those of his family and friends, in a desperate gesture of independence. Yet others, often including major religious figures, refuse to submit. They are shown no mercy. At the same time Ganji was taken back to prison in Tehran after his brave interview, six other political prisoners in Karaj Prison were starting their second week on hunger strikes, and eight others joined them. Three other political prisoners—Taghi Rahmani, Hoder Saber, and Reza-Ali Jani—smuggled a letter out of prison, addressed to outgoing "reformist" President Khatami, declaring that they had savagely been tortured. Rahmani said he had been held in solitary confinement for 134 days, and the others described humiliations I do not care to repeat here.

BATEBI

The face of the Iranian resistance is Ahmad Batebi, a student whose photograph appeared on the cover of *The Economist*, holding up the bloody T-shirt of a friend during the 1999 pro-democracy demonstrations in Tehran. He had already become one of the leaders of the student movement, but that photograph sealed his fate. He was rounded up and sentenced to death. The sentence was later reduced to a mere fifteen years in jail, more than a year of which was served in solitary confinement.

Any Iranian dissident who has been subjected to the rigors of the regime's jails will tell you that those who make it through form a community of survivors. So Batebi continued to organize a dissident network for several years and managed to send and receive letters by bribing his jailers.

Released on "furlough" in the spring of 2005, Batebi went underground, seeking to mobilize his friends and comrades for a major push against the regime before Ahmadinejad was sworn in as president, and the foreseeable crackdown on all forms of protest began.

Moving from house to house, communicating with his prisonmates by letters smuggled in and out of Evin, Batebi gave several interviews by cell telephone. "What I want is international pressure for all the political prisoners who have been so horribly treated. I want all these human rights activists, these Amnesty Internationals, to put their resources together to give more attention to the political prisoners in Iran."[7]

Rejecting the pleas of his overseas friends and supporters to get out of the country, Batebi was finally captured in the summer of 2006 and subjected to the

---

[7] Rachel Zabarkes Friedman, "Youngbloods," *National Review Online*, August 3, 2005.

harshest treatment. He did not break, nor did his torturers. On February 20, 2007, his friends and lawyer announced that Batebi had suffered a stroke the previous week. His lawyer reported that Batebi, in a coma, had been taken to a hospital near Evin Prison, and that doctors were not even permitted to examine him without the presence of security guards, so great was the fear that Batebi might escape a second time.

After minimal treatment, he was carried back to Evin, and shortly thereafter his wife was arrested, held for a week, then released. It was part of a broader pattern. In recent months, there had been a rising tempo of arrests and interrogations of student activists all over the country. A member of the central committee of the official student movement announced, "In the past month at least three hundred students have been summoned to disciplinary committees, and that number has actually increased with the new wave of summoning." He reported that seventy-five Tehran students at the University of Tehran had been summoned to disciplinary committees in the past month alone, an unprecedented level of repression in the history of the university.[8]

---

[8] Hasan Zarezade Ardeshir, "Jailed Student Leader Batebi Suffers Brain Stroke," *Roozonline*, February 20, 2007.

BOROUJERDI

Perhaps the most spectacular case of resistance to the regime is the story of Ayatollah Mohammed Kazemeini Boroujerdi, an Iranian cleric fighting against the "political religion" that has dominated his country since Khomeini.[9] Boroujerdi's challenge to the legitimacy of the Islamic Republic lasted several years. Both he and his father—who died in 2002 and whose grave has been desecrated—refused to embrace the Khomeinist doctrine that only a Shi'ite sage was fit to govern the Islamic Republic. The Boroujerdis retained the traditional Shi'ite view—the one famously held by Ayatollah Sistani in Iraq—that clerics should stay out of government and tend to their flocks.

Ayatollah Boroujerdi was in and out of prison and repeatedly in front of the Special Court for the Clergy, starting in 2003, barely a year after his father's death. According to Amnesty International, "he has reportedly developed heart and kidney problems as a result of torture."

His most celebrated round of defiance started in late June 2006, when he preached to a large crowd in a Tehran

---

[9] Michael A. Ledeen, "The Mullahs' Massacre on the Road to Qom," *Pajamas Media*, October 8, 2006.

sports stadium. A month later, on July 30, the secret police came to his house, intending to arrest him. But they found that he was protected by scores of supporters, so they arrested some of them instead. According to Amnesty International, one of the victims had a heart attack on the spot and was moved to a nearby hospital. Another said that he was arrested at his home and dragged off to three weeks of solitary confinement and daily threats.

The security forces tried again on August 3 and were again driven off by Boroujerdi's defenders. A month later, they tried a different approach. Boroujerdi was visited by a government security agent, to try to talk some sense into the ayatollah. So the world outside could understand the kind of intimidation used by the regime, even against high-ranking clerics such as Boroujerdi, he secretly taped the conversation, then had it smuggled out of Iran to the United States.[10]

The security agent began as a "good cop." He assured the ayatollah that he, too, was a religious man, having attended a seminary after the Revolution. He said that the visit was a kind of courtesy call, offering Boroujerdi the chance to surrender in a civilized way and then face trial. There is no escape possible, he said, for one way or another

---

[10] It was made available to me by Banafsheh Zand-Bonazzi, a leading Iranian-American activist who lives in New York City.

Boroujerdi would face charges of insulting the government and the clerisy, and perhaps even having been an accomplice to murder.

Boroujerdi would have none of it. He defiantly told the agent that he had already prepared himself for martyrdom (and indeed when he was finally arrested, he was wearing a funeral shroud). He added that he had already suffered a heart attack, did not fear death, and that he would now contact the foreign press. This enraged the agent, who warned Boroujerdi that no place would be safe for him, even the mosque. He confirmed Boroujerdi's dark suspicions that his father had been murdered by order of the regime and said that he didn't give a damn about the foreign press.

Boroujerdi did indeed contact the media and also wrote to such world leaders as Kofi Annan and Javier Solana, to their apparent indifference. Amnesty International, one of the few organizations to pay any attention to the story, only issued a press release about a month after Boroujerdi's conversation with the agent, and there was little coverage of it elsewhere.

The secret police came again for Boroujerdi on the morning of September 28, again found he was defended, and again dragged off many of his supporters. In its press release five days later, Amnesty wrote, with a rare flair for understatement, "There are fears that the Ayatollah may be at risk of imminent arrest."

Boroujerdi was dragged off to his destiny a few days later in a dramatic confrontation that involved thousands of demonstrators, some in Tehran, and some on the road to Qom, where many of the country's most prestigious religious schools and scholars are located. The official news media reported that more than two hundred supporters were arrested at the house in Tehran, but this was the least of it. The security forces (Revolutionary Guards) were unable to clear the road, since people from various towns joined the original protest. A violent confrontation occurred when Revolutionary Guards special units were called in. Several hundred were arrested, and many were hospitalized, including five Revolutionary Guardsmen in critical condition.

That such a demonstration could take place at all shows that opposition to the regime is quite widespread. It's hard to imagine a more direct attack against the regime; support for Boroujerdi, who opposed Khomeini's constitution and the requirement of a theocratic state, was tantamount to calling for the end of the Islamic Republic. Thousands of people stood up to the regime's killers, in defense of a solitary religious man whose crime was to preach traditional Shi'ite values. That's a major event.

No doubt many of the people on the highway to Qom were protesting the skyrocketing inflation that has taken place under the mullahs—and gotten considerably worse under Ahmadinejad—while others were challenging the regime for political reasons, because they wish to be free. But no matter which way you look at it, the willingness of Iranian citizens to risk life and limb to express their contempt for the mullahs is a major indicator of the internal political situation.

The Boroujerdi case is the tip of a large and perhaps counterintuitive dissident group that is rarely discussed in the press, although it is well-known to all informed Iranians: the growing clerical opposition to the Islamic Republic. In the holy city of Qom, thousands of clerics suffer in jail because they have criticized the regime, and Qom is usually the Iranian city with the lowest voter participation in the country's elections. The antiregime clerics are certainly not opposed to Shi'ism, let alone to Islam, but they are alarmed at the regime's failure, oppose the harsh oppression, and, reasonably enough, fear that when the regime comes down, Islam may gravely be weakened. In January 2007, the country's most senior dissident cleric, Grand Ayatollah Hossein Ali Montazeri, attacked the regime's policies, saying, "The people's economic problems cannot be resolved by chanting slogans," and called for the release of political prisoners.

The dissident clerics are right to be concerned because Islam is indeed losing followers in Iran. An Iranian ayatollah told me that it was not unusual to find the central mosque in major cities such as Shiraz and Tabriz virtually empty for Friday prayers. He said that a grand total of five people had shown up in Tabriz one Friday. The unpopularity of Islam is a major cause of opposition to the regime from some of the country's highest-ranking clerics, as well as students, intellectuals, workers, and teachers, because they see the steady erosion of the ideological basis for the Islamic Republic itself.

ZOROASTRIANS

Little noticed outside Iran, the decline of Islam has stimulated an underground revival of Zoroastrianism. Long afflicted by the Islamic Republic, Zoroastrianism remains an important unifying symbol for Iranians of all ethnic groups, as can be seen in the annual celebration of Norouz, the "Iranian" New Year. Both the importance of the celebration and the regime's great fear of such celebrations are regularly downplayed by the Western press. Just look at the Reuters coverage of the holiday in 2005:

ISFAHAN—Iranian authorities beat up and teargassed exuberant young revelers as they breathed new life into a pre-Islamic fire festival with a night of dancing, flirting, and fireworks. The Islamic Republic, which has an awkward relationship with its ancient Zoroastrian religion, only gave guarded recognition to the "Chaharshanbe Souri" festival last year.[11]

The Islamic Republic does not have "an awkward relationship" with Zoroastrianism. It restricts Zoroastrian practices, including the celebration of the Zoroastrian New Year, Norouz. Never mind "guarded recognition"; there is a fear. The mullahs know that a big Zoroastrian revival is under way in Iran, another sign of the hollowness of the Islamic Republic, and the hostility of the Iranian people to their leaders. And to say that the authorities "beat up and gassed" some "revelers" is quite an understatement, since, on the evening of March 15, there were large-scale demonstrations all over Iran, combining the Norouz celebrations with calls for the downfall of the regime itself. Effigies of top mullahs were burned in the streets. But Reuters makes it sound like a frat party that just got a bit out of hand:

Hundreds of people poured onto the streets in Tehran and other cities for a rare night of partying. Public revelry is unusual in Iran where the authorities consider it to be at odds with the country's strict moral codes.

---

[11] Quoted in Michael Ledeen, "The Fire in Iran," *National Review Online*, March 17, 2005.

The IRNA news agency said police used tear gas in more than four places in Tehran. Vigilantes were also seen beating up a group of boys in the central city of Isfahan.

In fact, the Tehran clashes were symptomatic of what was going on all over the country. Isfahan, Mahabad, Shiraz, Rasht, Kermanshah, Babol, Sannandaj, Dezful, Mashhad, Ahwaz, Marivan, Khorramabad, Zabol, Baneh, Tabriz, Hamedan and Oroomiah all experienced street fights between the regime's security forces and groups of Iranians.

No wonder, then, that the regime is moving ahead to destroy ancient monuments that remind the people of their pre-Islamic heritage. Just as the Taliban famously blew up the monumental statues of Buddha, Khomeini and his heirs planned to raze the remnants of the ancient Persian empires. Some of those plans are now being implemented. In late January 2007, the minister of power and energy announced that the Sivand Dam would begin operating, which would submerge the ruins of the capital city of Cyrus the Great. In case any Iranian had any doubts about the reason why, it was timed to coincide with a ten-day celebration of Khomeini's triumphal return to Iran in 1979.

The rulers of the Islamic Republic have thereby

managed to unify secular and religious opponents of the regime.

MINORITIES

Half of Iranians are Persian, and the other half are composed of various ethnic groups and tribes: Azeris, Kurds, Baluchi, Ahwazi Arabs, Lur, and so forth. Plus, a very small part of the population is non-Muslim, of which the Jews and the Baha'is are the best known, and the Zoroastrians are perhaps the largest. The mullahs view them all with hatred and suspicion, and they are constantly concerned about the security of their people. From time to time, ethnic-cleansing campaigns are launched against them, lately with particular intensity against the Ahwazis, Zoroastrians, and Baluchi. The campaign against the Kurds dates to the first months of the Islamic Republic and has never been stopped. In late February 2007, Ahmadinejad warned Iraq that his government would not hesitate to enter Iraqi territory to act against the Kurds if the Iraqis didn't prevent "their" Kurds from behaving in (unspecified) ways counter to Iranian wishes. This followed many months of joint Iranian-Turkish ground attacks against Kurds in northern Iraq.

In the south, the regime has been conducting a secret

ethnic-cleansing campaign against the Ahwazi Arabs. British human rights activist Peter Tatchell calls it "a sustained, bloody campaign of intimidation and persecution against its Arab minority,"[12] waged in secret to the great indifference of most of the world. It's the usual pattern. Sixteen Ahwazis were sentenced to death on the basis of confessions produced under torture, and the executions "seem designed to silence protests by Iran's persecuted ethnic Arabs." The government has announced plans to transfer a million Arabs to another region of the country, recalling Stalin's efforts to solve his "nationalities problem" by similar means.

Anyone trying to dig out the facts of the court cases runs up against a hard stone wall. "Foreign journalists are severely restricted and local reporters are intimidated with threats of imprisonment." Even so, some elements of this remarkable repression have filtered out. For one thing, all Ahwazi trade unions, student groups, and political parties have been banned. In the year starting October 2005, no less than a quarter of a million Arabs were moved from their villages, and another four hundred thousand are facing similar prospects in the near future. Dozens of towns and villages have been

---

[12] Peter Tatchell, "Tehran's Secret War Against Its Own People," *The Times* (London), October 10, 2006.

bulldozed into the sand. At the same time, Persians are offered interest-free loans to move into new towns in the vacated areas, and plans call for half a million to arrive in the near future. All Arab newspapers and schoolbooks have been banned, and all instruction is in Farsi (a pattern repeated in all minority ethnic areas). Eighty percent of Ahwazi children suffer from malnutrition, even though they live in the potentially richest area of the country; 90 percent of the oil comes from there.

Not that the regime's ethnic-cleansing campaign against the Ahwazis is simply the result of some sort of racist or cultural hatred per se; it has a decidedly geopolitical dimension: control of the Shatt al Arab, the narrow waterway between Iran and Iraq through which much of Iranian and Iraqi oil passes en route to major markets. If the Iranians can dominate the waterway—where fifteen British sailors and marines were taken hostage in March 2007—they can effectively dominate much of the Iraqi economy. The mullahs have therefore set about the construction of a major military stronghold in the area, and that in turn requires that the Ahwazis be removed. The regime simply kicks out the locals and transfers ownership of the land to the Iranian Revolutionary Guards Corps and state-owned enterprises. This has the pleasant side effect of enriching the mighty: some forty-seven thousand hectares of Ahwazi farmland were deeded over to favored businessmen and individual members of the security forces. The indigenous Ahwazis have been reduced to misery and forced into shantytowns.[13]

Similar treatment has been applied to the Azeris, Baluchi, Kurds, and other smaller groups. Despite Tehran's efforts to convince the world there is a real risk of ethnic separatism, and thus without tough action the country might be split apart (a concern often shared by diaspora Iranians in Europe and the United States), the ethnic groups are overwhelmingly patriotic and at most ask for moderate rights of the sort that have become common throughout Europe: dual language education, some media outlets in their traditional language, and the celebration of traditional holidays.

But the regime cannot risk granting even those mild freedoms. The regime in Tehran has long since lost any semblance of popular support and has maintained power only through the systematic use of terror against its people. It cannot claim popularity on the basis of its accomplishments, because twenty-eight years of theocracy have produced ruin and misery. More than four million people have fled the Revolution, most of them well educated and highly skilled. The data on those trapped by the tyrants

---

[13] Daniel Brett, "Iran's Imperial Project in the Shatt al-Arab," British Ahwazi Friendship Society, 2007.

are startling, but altogether in keeping with the Islamic Revolution's historical indifference to social misery. As Khomeini neatly summarized it, the revolution was about religion, "not about the price of watermelons."[14]

- Forty percent of the population lives below the poverty line according to the CIA's World Fact Book (2002).
- Unemployment is at least 15 percent and perhaps significantly higher, as compared to less than 3 percent in the last years of the Shah.
- Close to 4.5 million Iranians live on less than $1.25 per month according to Ahmadinejad deputy Parviz Dawoodi.
- In 2000 per capita income was 60 percent of what it was before the Revolution.
- Iranian economists estimate capital flight at up to $3 billion a year, and it may well be significantly greater, as those with money send it to safe havens abroad.[15]

---

[14] Ramin Mostaghim, "Iranian Bank Note Stirs Chain Reaction," *Los Angeles Times*, March 14, 2007. The headline is a rare pun on Iran's nuclear project.

[15] Reliable data are very hard to come by; these are drawn from publications by the CIA and the World Bank, from Iranian newspapers, and from blogs such as *Roozonline*.

• The distribution of the shrinking wealth is firmly in the hands of the regime's elite families. More than 80 percent of the country's gross national product comes from the petroleum industry, which is entirely in government hands. The mullahs have effectively ruined this primary source of national wealth: oil production is currently 3.9 million barrels per day, while it was 6.2 million at the end of the shah's rule. According to a study released on Christmas Day 2006 by the National Academy of Sciences, oil exports are expected to decline by upward of 10 percent a year for the foreseeable future.

• Inflation has run wild. The exchange rate was 70 rials to the dollar in '78, and it was about 9,300 in the spring of 2007, when a new 50,000-rial banknote (graced with an atomic symbol) was introduced.

• There are said to be more than fifty thousand suicides per year.

Europeans shun the country. In the summer of 2001, *Newsweek International* proclaimed Iran the "worst country in the world for journalists," and the French-led international organization *Reporters sans frontières* branded Ayatollah Khamenei the Middle East's leading "predator" of a free press. According to the organization, Iran ranks

162nd out of 168 countries in meeting internationally recognized standards of a free press.

All of this might have been tolerated in the name of the true faith if the leaders had demonstrated a virtuous asceticism. But the regime is famously corrupt and has instituted a unique form of state theft. A percentage of most business deals, and even many elementary cash transactions, is deposited in an account known as the "leadership's household," which is entirely at the disposal of the Supreme Leader, the Ayatollah Ali Khamenei. This tax ranges upward from about 5 percent to nearly 30 percent on luxury items. The base price for a standard Iranian car—the Peykan—is roughly $6,250 but the actual cost is $8,125. The difference goes to Khamenei. The leadership is awash in money while the people starve.

Most Iranians are convinced that the ruling class is enormously corrupt, and with good reason. The average salary for an Iranian minister is less than $500 a month, and it is impossible for such a person to live on such a salary; he is getting additional money elsewhere. Every now and then the curtain is lifted a tiny bit, and the corrupt practices are exposed. In 2002 a young financial wheeler-dealer by the name of Shahram Jazayeri-Arab was sentenced to twenty-seven years in jail for paying bribes to government officials in exchange for big contracts. His conviction was "partially canceled" and he was scheduled for a new trial in early 2007. But he mysteriously disappeared from Evin Prison before the trial started. He apparently got out of the country before all security and police forces received the instruction to arrest him.

Jazayeri's escape was a major event and produced major consequences: the immediate purge of the director of Evin Prison, the director of the judiciary branch responsible for combating economic corruption, and two judges involved in his case.[16] The escape was clearly orchestrated, since Jazayeri apparently knew an awful lot about powerful people who were on the take.

The most scandalous aspect of the case is the extensive connection of Jazayeri with the children of senior conservative clerics, commonly known as the Aghazadehs—which in Persian means the children of prominent gentlemen. This issue was so serious that soon after the corruption case was officially filed, the head of Iran's judiciary stressed that he would pursue the violations of the children of senior clerics and announced, "We would pursue the Aghazadehs cases by starting our investigation with those closest to us."

At about the same time, an informed judiciary authority told *Iran* newspaper (May 1, 2002) that regarding

---

[16] Hossein Bastani, "The Hidden Half of Jazaeri's Case," *Roozonline*, March 9, 2007.

the charges of having monetary connections with (the son of Iran's former attorney general) and (the son of Iran's former minister of intelligence), Shahram Jazayeri has said that the son of another prominent official involved in the scandal was (the son of a former member of the Guardian Council). The then secretary of the Islamic Coalition Party, Habibollah Asgharoladi, said the following in this connection: "The case is clear. He had purchased a ship and sold it to two or three separate buyers."

One nice touch spoke volumes about Iranians' view of their regime: Supreme Leader Khamenei had received a million dollars from Jazayeri, but returned it. So profound is the cynicism in Iran with regard to its leaders, it was widely believed that this did not demonstrate virtue on the part of the Supreme Leader, but only that Khamenei had been warned that there was evidence about the million dollars, enabling him to get rid of the money in time to escape any embarrassment.

As usual in such cases, the evidence against the regime was blamed on foreign conspiracies, and in the Jazayeri saga, the regime's apologists claimed that the bribes had come from overseas in order to entrap the recipients. This magically transformed corrupt officials into naïve victims of sly foreign enemies of the regime, and Jazayeri himself was portrayed as an enemy agent. He made lots of overseas phone calls, especially to Great Britain; he received loans from British and French banks; and he paid off some of his "victims" through "third-party intermediaries."

However, Jazayeri did not take refuge in the countries accused of sponsoring his illegal activities. On March 17, 2007, Iranian radio announced he had been arrested in "an Arab country" and would be extradited to Iran.

As Paul Klebnikov, the intrepid American journalist who specialized in exposing the Mafia-like activities of post–Soviet Russia—and was gunned down in Moscow in July 2004—wryly observed, "The economy bears more than a little resemblance to the crony capitalism that sprouted from the wreck of the Soviet Union. The 1979 revolution expropriated the assets of foreign investors and the nation's wealthiest families; oil had long been nationalized, but the mullahs seized virtually everything else of value—banks, hotels, car and chemical companies, makers of drugs and consumer goods."[17]

Despite Khomeini's celebrated contempt for earthly wealth, the ruling class of the Islamic Republic has demonstrated great avidity for both money and power. The most infamous case is the former president Ayatollah Ali Akbar Hashemi Rafsanjani, one of the country's most

---

[17] Paul Klebnikov, "Millionaire Mullahs," *Forbes*, July 21, 2003.

successful politicians and businessmen, the chairman of the Council of Experts, which names the Supreme Leader, and at this writing a leading contender to succeed the ailing Ali Khamenei, the successor to Khomeini.

Rafsanjani used the privatization program he launched during his presidency to redistribute state-owned enterprises to friends, political allies, and his own family members. The Rafsanjanis were pistachio farmers, and one of Hashemi's brothers now runs a big pistachio export business, estimated at roughly half a billion dollars per year. If you buy pistachios in Iranian-American shops in southern California (especially in "Terangeles"), the odds are long that you will be enriching the Rafsanjani family.

The Rafsanjanis' empire was built on the destruction of the old order. Shortly after the Revolution, family members gobbled up the national television network, created import/export companies, took key positions in the Petroleum Ministry and the organization that builds and manages the Tehran subway system, and even acquired a thirty-acre horse farm in an upscale neighborhood in the capital (where, according to Klebnikov, land now sells for a cool $4 million per acre). All this activity enabled the Rafsanjanis to leverage their hard currency, which they could buy for 1,750 rials per dollar (the subsidized rate for legitimate imports), then sell on the open market for 8,000 rials or more, depending on demand.

All that money translates into great political power in a country where most people are struggling to make ends meet. Favors are granted and purchased, networks are established, and the ability to conduct business on an international scale means that money can be salted away in foreign banks as insurance against bad days ahead. Other members of the theocratic ruling class have performed similarly, if less ostentatiously, especially those fortunate enough to have gained control over the national charities or the *bonyads*, powerful foundations that were in many cases originally created by the shah's family and were seized after the Revolution. All operate under the direct control of the Supreme Leader. The most famous of these is the Mostazafan and Jambazan Foundation, long managed by Mohsen Rafiqdoost, whose main credential was his role as Khomeini's chauffeur on the imam's triumphal entry into Tehran after the fall of the shah. From there he became minister of the Revolutionary Guards, then head of the Mostazafan Foundation, then the Noor Foundation, another Islamic "charity" that runs big real estate ventures, imports medicines and other pharmaceutical products, and dabbles in the construction business.

All of this activity generates enormous sums of money, a large part of which is spent on international terrorism and the country's secret nuclear project. In Klebnikov's words, Iran today is "a dictatorship run by a shadow government that—the U.S. State Department suspects—finances terrorist groups abroad through a shadow foreign policy. Its economy is dominated by shadow business empires and its power is protected by a shadow army of enforcers."

Inevitably, the Revolutionary Guards—the main instrument of terror both inside Iran and in the international arena—realized that it would be more efficient to take direct control over a significant part of the business activities that, after all, provided them with much of their budget. Last year, the deputy commander of the IRGC gave a rare public interview in which he admitted that nearly one-third of the Guards' operations were not military at all, but commercial. Estimates of annual earnings run into the billions of dollars, most likely tens of billions.[18] According to information from well-informed Iranians, as of the start of Operation Iraqi Freedom, the Revolutionary Guards controlled more than thirty companies in Iran and Dubai, through which most of the funding for foreign terrorist operations flowed.

The current Iranian president, Mahmoud Ahmadinejad, is a creature of the Revolutionary Guards. His elevation was due in large part to their power and wealth, and

---

[18] Najmeh Bozorgmehr and Gareth Smyth, "Military Force Finds Its Wealth Under Attack," *Financial Times*, March 16, 2007.

he has ensured that their wealth will increase. As the *Financial Times* tells us, he managed to award the Guards several big contracts: a gas pipeline from the Gulf, an exploration contract for a major gas field, and the construction of a new line for the Tehran subway.

As of the spring of 2007, Ahmadinejad and Rafsanjani were engaged in a very public fight for the right to succeed Khamenei, then struggling against a particularly virulent cancer. That fight was not just over which of them would be the next Supreme Leader (and it was by no means certain that the two names exhausted the candidate pool); it was also over enormous sums of money, and therefore over great political power.

One thing was certain: whoever succeeded Khamenei was unlikely to change the basic international strategy of the Islamic Republic. That had been established by the Imam Khomeini within weeks of the seizure of power in February 1979, and the mullahs believed it was succeeding.

2 THE IRANIAN WAR PLAN

Al Qaeda . . . forged alliances with the National Islamic Front in the Sudan and with the government of Iran and its associated terrorist group Hezbollah for the purpose of working together against their perceived common enemies in the West, particularly the United States.

—From the indictment of Osama bin Laden et al.
by the U.S. government in 1998

As I looked at the evidence in front of me . . . the Islamic Republic of Iran had declared a secret war against the United States.

—Robert Baer, former CIA case officer

The Prophet Muhammad famously wrote to several infidel leaders inviting them to convert to Islam as the only reliable way to ensure the security of their domains. These letters were sent to the rulers of Egypt, Ethiopia, Persia, and Byzantium, among others. The letters—some of which have survived the centuries—

were often a prelude to armed attack, but in all cases conveyed Muhammad's conviction that the recipient was doomed unless he accepted God's truth as revealed in the Quran.

The practice was revived by the Islamic Republic of Iran, which, like the Prophet, aspired to global ascendance. Six months before his death in 1989, the Ayatollah Khomeini wrote a similar letter to Mikhail Gorbachev; a leading Iranian cleric wrote in a similar vein to Fidel Castro; and in mid-2006, President Mahmoud Ahmadinejad wrote an eight-page message to President George W. Bush. The Iranian president pronounced Western-style liberal democracy a failure, declared Bush a hypocrite, and invited him to convert.

The letter to Bush closes with a famous phrase in Arabic: *Vasalam ala man ataba'al hoda*, meaning "Peace unto those who follow the true path,"[1] the same words with which Muhammad closed his messages to the Byzantine and Persian emperors. In both cases, Muhammad's letters were preludes to war. In short, the Prophet offered a choice of Islam or the sword to the infidels.

Ahmadinejad was simply restating the unstinting

---

[1] *The New York Sun* (May 11, 2006, editorial) translated it as "peace *only* unto those . . ."

enmity that the Islamic Republic had always reserved for the United States. Not a week had passed since the 1979 Revolution in which some leading cleric had not led the faithful in chants of "Death to America!" and not a year had passed without subversive actions against Islamic regimes viewed by Tehran as American friends or allies. The inclusion of the historic words in the original language was aimed at the Islamic world, a reminder that Iran considered itself the legitimate leader of the worldwide community of believers.

Khomeini set out at once to establish Iranian hegemony over the Muslim Middle East, entrusting the details of this vital task to his designated successor, Ayatollah Hossein Ali Montazeri. In short order, the region was shaken by a series of spectacular events, often timed to take place within days or even hours of each other. This pattern became a calling card of the mullahs and was later repeated by Al Qaeda.

The first sequence began on November 4, 1979, with the seizure of the American embassy in Tehran, the capture of American embassy personnel, and an international crisis that lasted 444 days, the remainder of the Carter presidency. On November 20, four hundred "pilgrims" on the hajj in Mecca occupied the Grand Mosque, taking several hundred hostages, calling for the overthrow of the ruling Saudi royal family, and the end of all ties to the West. The

Grand Mosque became a battleground, and it took two weeks of tough fighting—and some 250 dead, including scores of Saudi National Guardsmen, and hundreds wounded—to reestablish order. It was widely rumored that French and Jordanian Special Forces had helped defeat the Iranian-sponsored assault on one of the holiest sites in the Islamic world (it was said that the French commandos received an instant conversion to Islam so that they could enter the holy place). Sixty-seven participants were captured and beheaded.

The assault on the Grand Mosque had a significant footnote: the first appearance of the name bin Laden in conjunction with a terrorist attack. Osama bin Laden's brother Mahrous was apparently involved in the operation and was miraculously spared the executioner's scimitar. He even gained early release from prison, abandoned political activism, and subsequently devoted all his energies to the family business.[2]

Iran immediately blamed the United States for the desecration of the mosque, and the following day a mob assaulted the American embassy in Pakistan. Five days thereafter, fearing that assaults on American property in

---

[2] For the story of Osama's brother, see *Sunday Herald* (Glasgow), October 7, 2001; *Ha'aretz*, December 18, 2002; and *The New Yorker*, November 5, 2001.

the Middle East would become endemic, all nonessential U.S. diplomatic personnel were evacuated from ten Muslim countries. Then, on the twenty-ninth of November, there were monster riots by openly pro-Iranian Shi'ites in Hasa, Saudi Arabia. One hundred fifty-six people were killed in the fighting.

The apogee of Iranian action against the Saudi royal family's control of the Muslim holy sites in Mecca and Medina came in the summer of 1987, during the annual hajj that all Muslims are required to undertake at least once in their lives. Prior to their departure from Iran, the pilgrims received an injunction from Supreme Leader Khomeini to avoid any violence or even disputes or insults. There had often been anti-Saudi and pro-Khomeini demonstrations in the past, with pilgrims chanting, "Islam is one, Khomeini is leader."

On July 31 hundreds of Iranian pilgrims rioted, denouncing the "enemies of Islam" and challenging the Saudi police, who traditionally maintained order during the ritual. During the ensuing conflict, more than 400 pilgrims were killed, and nearly 650 wounded. Khomeini responded the next day with calls for the overthrow of the Saudi royal family. Over a million Iranians were mobilized in Tehran to repeat Khomeini's demand, and the Kuwaiti and Saudi embassies in Tehran were assaulted by mobs.

The riots and demonstrations followed a dark period in the history of the Islamic Republic. Twenty thousand Iranian soldiers had been killed by nerve gas deployed by Saddam's armies three months before; six weeks later American naval forces sank two Iranian frigates and several armed speedboats in the Persian Gulf; and just a few days before the hajj riots, an Iranian airliner was accidentally shot down by missiles from the USS *Vincennes*, killing nearly three hundred passengers and crew. These events compelled Khomeini to call an end to the Iran-Iraq War on unfavorable terms, a decision he described as "swallowing bitter poison." In all likelihood, Khomeini had authorized the hajj riots hoping to demonstrate Iran's regional outreach, and widespread support throughout the Muslim world. Instead, it provoked disgust in most Islamic countries.

The mullahs also sponsored more traditional acts of political subversion and murder on a global scale. Thanks to the fecklessness of the West in the face of brutal ethnic conflict in the Balkans, the Iranians were permitted to send weapons to Islamic radicals in Bosnia, an opening they exploited by creating a network of terrorist training camps throughout the area. They supported attempted coups in the early eighties in Qatar and Bahrain, at the same time kidnapping and murdering Americans in Lebanon and assassinating political dissidents and representatives of the shah's regime in Western Europe. Iranian-sponsored terrorists killed hundreds of Argentinians in two huge car-bomb attacks in the nineties, along with large numbers of Americans in Saudi Arabia. In league with Al Qaeda, the mullahs killed hundreds of innocents in American embassies in East Africa.

THE WEAPONS OF WAR

The two main instruments for most of this mayhem were the Revolutionary Guards—especially its overseas arm, the Quds Force—and Hezbollah, "Allah's Party", which was created by Iran in Lebanon in the early eighties and received additional military protection and logistical support from the Syrian dictatorship of the Assad family. It eventually became the one real success of the mullahs' dream of creating Islamic republics outside Iran.

Like so many terrorist organizations, Hezbollah was organized and trained by the Iranian Revolutionary Guards Corps (IRGC, or more simply, the RG). Most of the training took place in Lebanon itself, where the Revolutionary Guards were created in the early 1970s, and where Hezbollah would later carry out some of its most infamous operations.[3] The IRGC was created in Lebanon's Bekáa Valley, by Al-Fatah, the armed wing of Yasir Arafat's PLO. According to one of the Iranian leaders present for much of that period,[4] the working relationship between Khomeini and Arafat began at least as early as 1972, seven full years before the Iranian Revolution. Fatah carried out a training program for the Iranian paramilitary units that were officially designated as the RG following the overthrow of the shah (to which they contributed mightily, from killing followers of the old regime to maintaining order and discipline among the variegated elements of Khomeini's coalition). The Revolutionary Guards were first used by Khomeini to conduct paramilitary operations against the shah, then as a Praetorian Guard to impose the ayatollah's will on the Iranian people, and finally as a parallel military and intelligence force for both domestic and foreign purposes.

Some have suggested that the RG constituted a "state

---

[3] One of the Iranians in charge of the creation of Hezbollah was Qassem Asgari, who disappeared from Istanbul in February 2007. As of this writing, there was no reliable information on why or how Asgari vanished, or whether he had been kidnapped or had defected.

[4] I have spent many hours with this man, who was subsequently accused of treason by the Islamic Republic, tortured in Evin Prison in Tehran, and miraculously escaped Iran. He now lives in a Western country.

within the state," but it is more accurate to say that it has long been one of the state's central domestic and foreign weapons. Clare Lopez, a longtime CIA operations officer who was the executive director of the Iran Policy Committee, put it bluntly: "Iran's Revolutionary Guards *are* the regime."[5] It was automatic for Khomeini to use the RG to train and command Hezbollah's killers; they shared the same ideological and operational DNA. The RG was the biological father of Hezbollah. The RG's genetic code remains a constant in Tehran: Supreme Leader Ali Khamenei was president of the Islamic Republic from 1981 to 1989 and was therefore intimately involved in the Guards' operations during the Iran-Iraq War. President Mahmoud Ahmadinejad was an RG commander during the war and subsequently became a senior commander in the IRGC's Quds Force.[6] There is therefore a direct chain of command from the Supreme Leader and the president through the Revolutionary Guards to Hezbollah.

Although it was created as a political party with an extensive charitable network years before the Iranian

---

[5] Clare M. Lopez, "Iran's Revolutionary Guards ARE the Regime," *American Thinker*, February 22, 2007.

[6] Dan Diker, "President Bush and the Quds Force Controversy: Lessons Learned," Institute for Contemporary Affairs, *Jerusalem Issue Brief 6*, no. 22 (March 6, 2007).

Revolution, Hezbollah literally burst into public attention on April 18, 1983, when it bombed the U.S. embassy in Beirut. Sixty-three people were killed, including seventeen Americans, eight of whom were employees of the Central Intelligence Agency, including chief Middle East analyst Robert C. Ames and station chief Kenneth Haas. Barely six months later Hezbollah carried out simultaneous suicide bomb attacks on the barracks of both the U.S. and French marines in the same city. Two hundred forty-one U.S. marines were killed, and more than one hundred others were wounded.

The marriage between Hezbollah and Iran was perfect for both of them. They had a near total identity of ideological conviction. As one of Hezbollah's more reflective activists wrote just a couple of years ago, the most important elements of their joint worldview were:

- A belief in the Khomeinist doctrine, according to which there should be a devout wise man at the top of the state, and for the moment that man was Khomeini himself.
- The creation of an Islamic republic under a rigorous system of Sharia law.
- "Absolute rejection of superpower hegemony, the safeguarding of independence, and support for all

the liberation movements" (which is to say, all-out war against America and Israel, through total support for any and all terrorist groups, of whatever religious or nonreligious description).[7]

From the outset, the operational chief of Hezbollah has been Imad Mughniyah, a Lebanese Shi'ite who grew up in the Shi'ite neighborhoods of south Beirut and was recruited into Yasir Arafat's Al-Fatah. Prior to Osama bin Laden, Mughniyah was America's Most Wanted Man. He organized the Beirut massacres, masterminded the kidnapping of the CIA's Beirut station chief William Buckley in 1984, and participated in the fifteen months of torture that killed the American spymaster. In 1985 he personally murdered the American navy diver Robert Stethem, a passenger on a TWA flight from Athens to Beirut that was hijacked by two Hezbollah terrorists, and tossed Stethem's body onto the tarmac at the Beirut airport.

Mughniyah's transition from a foot soldier in the PLO—a largely secular terrorist organization that had grown out of the (Sunni) Muslim Brotherhood—to the Iranians' top killer is another instance of the ease

---

[7] Naim Qassem, *Hizbullah: The Story from Within* (London: SAQI, 2005).

with which Sunnis and Shi'ites have cooperated to kill their common Western enemies. The slaughter of the Americans in Beirut in 1983 involved both Iranian Shi'ite and PLO Sunni resources, which by then was an old story.

Iran's assault continued in the winter of 1983, with a series of attacks in Kuwait. The targets ranged from the American and French embassies to the main oil refinery, the airport control tower, and a residential neighborhood heavily populated by employees of Raytheon, the American corporation involved in military support for the kingdom. Six people died and more than eighty were injured. The attacks were organized by an Iranian-supported group, Al Dawa, "The Call." Seventeen terrorists, including a relative of Mughniyah's, were arrested and condemned to death or extended jail sentences. They subsequently became known as "the Dawa 17." The close connection between Iran and Hezbollah was repeatedly demonstrated when, throughout the eighties, Hezbollah took Western hostages and offered to trade them for the seventeen terrorists on death row in Kuwait. They tried hard indeed, as the world learned in December 1984 when a Kuwaiti passenger airliner was hijacked and flown to Tehran:

Most of the shades were tightly drawn, and there were few signs of life within. But Kuwaitis monitoring air-to-ground radio broadcasts picked up bloodcurdling sounds from the jet: they were the anguished shrieks and hysterical crying of a man being tortured and maimed. For those watching the tense drama developing, there were glimpses of gun-toting youths with checkered Arab headcloths drawn over their faces, and then the gruesome evidence of the hell unfolding for the 161 passengers and crew inside the grounded Airbus: the body of an American, stripped of all identifying papers, ignominiously dumped on the snow-dusted tarmac.[8]

The hijackers demanded the release of the Dawa terrorists in Kuwait, but the Kuwaitis refused even to discuss the matter. Two American hostages—unfortunate employees of USAID—were killed by the terrorists. Iranian security forces stormed the plane and arrested the terrorists. The Iranians promised to prosecute the culprits, but no trial was ever held.

Just three months earlier, on September 20, 1984, Hezbollah carried out the suicide bombing of the U.S. embassy annex on the outskirts of Beirut, killing twenty-four people (two of whom were Americans).

By the early nineties, Hezbollah and their Iranian

---

[8] John Kohan, "Horror Aboard Flight 221," *Time*, December 17, 1984.

terror masters had developed a global network. In 1992, they bombed the Israeli embassy in Buenos Aires, Argentina, and two years later in 1994 they bombed the city's biggest Jewish community center, killing 95 and wounding at least 151. It was the most horrific attack in the country's history (and Argentina had long been subjected to terrorist attacks).

The evidence against Iran and Hezbollah in the 1994 bombing took many years to assemble, and the formal accusation, with attendant arrest warrants, was only issued in the fall of 2006. The first ten years were spent on a failed prosecution of Argentines who were said to have been involved in handling payoffs by the Iranians to then-president Carlos Menem. When the case fell apart—leading to the impeachment of the investigating magistrate a year later—two federal prosecutors revived the investigation. Given access to secret intelligence files, the two developed a theory that Iran had ordered the attacks because Argentina first suspended and then terminated its support for the Iranian nuclear program (the Argentines had provided low-grade uranium and technical advice), as well as arms sales to the Islamic Republic. This theory came from someone who was in a position to know: a former Iranian intelligence officer named Abdolghassem Mesbahi.

Within a year, the investigation produced the identity of the bomber, a Hezbollah terrorist from Lebanon to whom a memorial plaque was dedicated in southern Lebanon. The plaque dated his "martyrdom" to July 18, 1994, which was the date of the bombings in Buenos Aires. The FBI, with whom the Argentinean prosecutors were working, came to the same conclusion.

The formal accusation came in late October 2006 and identified the government of Iran—through Hezbollah, which the report described as "from all points of view, a suborganization of the regime in Tehran"—as the guilty party.

Among the former Iranian officials cited in the report:

- President Hashemi Rafsanjani
- Intelligence Minister Ali Fallahian
- Foreign Minister Ali Akbar Velayati
- Mohsen Rezai, commander of the IRGC
- Mohsen Rabbani, cultural attaché to the Iranian embassy in Argentina (1994–98)
- Ahmad Reza Ashgari, third secretary of the Iranian embassy
- Ahmad Vahidi, commander of the Quds Force, 1989–98, and of course
- Hezbollah "Security Chief" Imad Mughniyah

The accusations were upheld by a federal magistrate, who issued arrest warrants and asked Interpol and the Iranian government to extradite them for judgment. When there was no response from the Iranians, Argentina demanded that the former Iranian officials be declared fugitives from justice and be placed on Interpol's list of wanted criminals. One of the prosecutors went to France to convince Interpol to issue international arrest warrants, only to be threatened by Iranian representatives with such vehemence that he feared for his own security.

In the end, Interpol agreed to list all but Rafsanjani and Velayati on their "watch list," while the Iranian regime blamed the whole thing on one of their favorite targets: in the words of a government spokesman, "The . . . indictments stem from Zionist political objectives."[9]

At the same time that the Iranians were unleashing Hezbollah on Jewish targets in Argentina, they were also establishing a working relationship with Al Qaeda. In 1993, Imad Mughniyah met with Osama bin Laden in Sudan. Bin Laden had been impressed with the suicide bombing of the American embassy in Beirut ten years earlier and wanted help in planning similar operations. The two agreed they

---

[9] The best source for the story is the Argentinean newspaper *Perfil*, www.Perfil.com, February 20, 2007.

would work together. Subsequently, Hezbollah trained Al Qaeda terrorists in Lebanon, Iran, and Sudan. It is fair to say that a great deal of Al Qaeda's methods, technology, and worldview came from the Islamic Republic, primarily from Mughniyah.

The presence of Sudan may come as a surprise to many readers, but it is a recurring theme in the history of Iran's early efforts to export the Islamic Revolution. As early as 1991 the two countries established a strategic alliance to wage war against their common enemies in the West, to overthrow pro-Western regimes in the Middle East, and to drive the Americans out of the region. Notice that the alliance bound Shi'ite Iran and Sunni Sudan, once again demonstrating the flimsiness of the Sunni/Shi'ite divide.

Indeed, the necessity of overcoming the mutual suspicion and hatred that divided some members of the two communities was a central theme of the Sudanese regime's "consigliere," Hassan al Turabi, an urbane, well-educated intellectual who for a while became a global celebrity. He met with the pope, spoke to a congressional subcommittee, was welcomed by a prestigious Washington think tank, and rose to star status in the European press, which nicknamed him "the Islamic Pope." Turabi was unique, a radical jihadist who also spoke the language of the Western intelligentsia. He publicly endorsed all manner of social reforms, including freeing women from the requirement of covering their hair ("they should cover their chest"), and sounded far more modern than any of his more infamous allies, from bin Laden to the leaders of Hezbollah. "Modern Islamic movements don't believe in schools of jurisprudence," he proclaimed in a lecture in Madrid in 1994, "they don't define themselves as Shia, or Sunni, or of this Sufi order or that Sufi order. They recognize this as quite a heritage and they can learn a lot from such history. They don't want to break with history altogether, but they want to go forward and develop."[10]

The smooth tones of moderation were terms of art, designed to deceive the West about his real intentions. In his own Sudan, all traditional political parties, along with anyone who dissented from the rigid Sharia code imposed on the nation, were brutally suppressed. As his celebrity increased, Turabi's dreams became ever more ambitious, but he was a big man on a tiny playing field and needed help to move into the global arena. Mere deception of gullible Westerners was not enough; he needed an army, and to that end he found willing part-

---

[10] Hassan al Turabi, "Islamic Fundamentalism in the Sunni and Shia Worlds" (lecture, Madrid, August 2, 1994), http://www.islamfortoday .com/turabi02.htm.

ners in the megalomaniacal rulers of the Islamic Republic. As the right arm of the Sudanese dictator, General Bashir, Turabi was able to make Sudan a central piece in the Iranian-led terror mosaic. The Iranians arrived in force, some to manage the decaying petroleum infrastructure, others to supervise training for a new military, still others—these from the feared and omnipresent Revolutionary Guards—to run numerous terrorist training camps. In 1993, a few hundred RG troops were working in Sudan; two years later, there were thousands of Iranian-trained terrorist trainers, some from the Revolutionary Guards and its Quds Force, many others from Hezbollah. The seriousness of the undertaking was proven by the presence of Hezbollah's operational chieftain, Imad Mughniyah, along with a new ally: Osama bin Laden. As the U.S. indictment of bin Laden stated in 1998, "Al Qaeda . . . forged alliances with the National Islamic Front in the Sudan and with the government of Iran and its associated terrorist group Hezbollah for the purpose of working together against their perceived common enemies in the West, particularly the United States."

The alliance between Sudan and Iran made perfectly good sense for the two Islamic fascist regimes, for they had a common overriding objective: to drive the United States out of the Middle East and destroy Israel. The sound logic of the alliance is proven by its durability. Iranian president Ahmadinejad recently visited Khartoum, where he embraced Sudanese president al-Bashir, an outspoken supporter of the Iranian nuclear program, and the driving force behind his army's genocidal war against the black, non-Muslim peoples of the south. "As if the symbolism of forging an alliance with a genocidal regime were not enough, Mr. Ahmadinejad declared to a group of Islamic scholars and officials in Khartoum that the 'Zionists are the true manifestation of Satan' and was greeted with chants of 'God is Great!'"[11]

In like manner, the working relationship between Al Qaeda and Hezbollah was equally logical. The two terrorist groups shared the broader strategic objectives, and there was good reason to share tactical and technological knowledge as well. Hezbollah had led the terror army that drove the United States out of Lebanon in 1984. Bin Laden was enormously impressed and wanted to learn from the warriors who had won that great Islamic victory. In addition, Al Qaeda wanted to stage spectacular attacks, of the sort Mughniyah had carried out in Lebanon, but lacked the technology to design the shaped charges needed to bring down big buildings.

---

[11] Thomas Cushman, "Only a Matter of Time . . . ," *The New York Sun*, March 29, 2007.

Bin Laden knew Mughniyah was a master of such attacks, wanted to learn how to do them, and got the necessary expertise, along with considerable wherewithal, from Hezbollah.

There is considerable documentation of the alliance among Iran, Sudan, Al Qaeda, and Hezbollah; some of it comes firsthand from Al Qaeda members who were involved in the African embassy bombings. From them, we learn that the first discussion was chaired by bin Laden himself in Khartoum and involved a "Sheikh Nomani," a representative of the Islamic Republic in Khartoum, a man known to have access to the top people in Tehran.[12] In keeping with the need to forge a working alliance against their common enemy, both sides promised to ignore any and all potentially divisive issues. An Al Qaeda member who was present at the first meeting made it luminously clear when he confessed to his terrorist activities:

Q: Can you tell us what was discussed at that meeting?

A: They talk about we have to come together and we have to forget the problem between each other and each one he should respect the other because our en-

---

[12] Rohan Gunaratna, *Inside Al Qaeda* (Penguin Group, 2003), 195.

emy is one and because there is no reason to fight each other.

Q: Who did they describe the enemy as being?

A: They say Westerns.[13]

As the relationship developed, the Iranians provided more important people, including Mughniyah. Testimony to this effect comes from the confession of Ali Mohamed, a onetime American army officer who joined Al Qaeda and participated in the bombing of the U.S. embassies in Tanzania and Kenya in 1998.

I was aware of certain contacts between Al Qaeda and [Egyptian Islamic] al Jihad organization, on one side, and Iran and Hezbollah on the other side. I arranged security for a meeting in the Sudan between Mughniyah, Hezbollah's chief, and bin Laden.

Hezbollah provided explosives training for Al Qaeda and al Jihad. Iran supplied Egyptian Jihad with weapons. Iran also used Hezbollah to supply explosives that were disguised to look like rocks.[14]

---

[13] http://cns.miis.edu/pubs/reports/pdfs/binladen/060201.pdf.
[14] http://cryptome.org/usa-v-mohamed.htm.

Similar explosives, some of them traced back to Iran, were used on Iraqi roads a decade later to attack coalition forces. In the interim, as the 9/11 Commission tells us, Al Qaeda terrorists were trained in Lebanon, Sudan, and Iran by Hezbollah and the Revolutionary Guards. The conversations in Sudan "led to an . . . agreement to [provide support] . . . for actions carried out primarily against Israel and the United States." Henceforth, Al Qaeda and Hezbollah worked together closely, sometimes in tandem with the Iranian Revolutionary Guards Corps, sometimes with experts from the MOIS, the Iranian intelligence ministry. "Both Hezbollah trainers and experts from Iran's Ministry of Information and Security trained Al Qaeda fighters in Sudan (in existing Al Qaeda facilities), Lebanon (in Hezbollah camps), and Iran (in officially run bases). Thereafter Al Qaeda's modus operandi came to resemble closely that of Hezbollah."[15]

The Al Qaeda–Iran tandem was made possible by the Sudanese regime, and Turabi's embrace of the Islamic Republic was well-known to the other governments of the region, and to American and European journalists working in the area. As early as January 1992, *The New York*

---

[15] *9/11 Commission Report*, 61.

Times flatly accused Sudan and Iran of "orchestrating . . . the spread of fundamentalism to the moderate Arab countries and the rest of Africa."[16]

Egyptian president Hosni Mubarak was understandably concerned, as he saw two of his country's terror groups—Egyptian Islamic Jihad and the Islamic Group—join the network, train alongside Al Qaeda and Hezbollah, and carry out operations in Egypt (Sadat was assassinated in 1981 by a team from Islamic Jihad). In time, the leader of Islamic Jihad, Dr. Ayman al-Zawahiri, signed up with bin Laden and became the number two figure in the organization.

Mubarak did everything he could to get the Americans' attention, even directly warning the director of central intelligence, James Woolsey. He told Woolsey that terrorism was getting worse in Egypt primarily because the terrorists were getting help from Iran, via Sudan.[17] His concerns were well-known to every American official who worked on Egyptian matters. Just look at the State Department's annual publication on international terrorism for the year 2000: "The Egyptian Government

---

[16] Jane Perlez, "A Fundamentalist Finds a Fulcrum in Sudan," *The New York Times*, January 29, 1992.
[17] Douglas Jehl, "Egypt Warns CIA Chief on Iran-Backed Terror," *The New York Times*, April 18, 1993.

believes that Iran, Bin Laden, and Afghan militant groups support [the Islamic Group]," and "the Egyptian Government claims that both Iran and bin Laden support [the Egyptian Islamic Jihad]."

It was even worse than that; Mubarak believed that the Sudanese government had organized an assassination attempt against him in 1995.

Meanwhile, Iran and its terrorist allies continued their war against the United States. The Khobar Towers military residence in Saudi Arabia was bombed on June 25, 1996, followed two years later by the near simultaneous bombings of the American embassies in Kenya and Tanzania. The Iranian role in Khobar Towers was recently confirmed in federal district court in Washington, D.C., where Judge Royce Lamberth laid out the evidence, which is worth reviewing at some length, as it well summarizes much of our understanding of the Iranian-sponsored terror network. Moreover, a lot of it has been repeated in the terror war in Iraq:

> The attack was carried out by individuals recruited principally by a senior official of [the Iranian Islamic Revolutionary Guards Corps], who . . . planned the operation and recruited individuals for the operation at the Iranian embassy in Damascus, Syria. He provided the passports,

the paperwork, and the funds for the individuals who carried out the attack. . . .

The truck bomb was assembled at a terrorist base in the Bekáa Valley which was jointly operated by the IRGC and by the terrorist organization known as Hezbollah. The individuals recruited to carry out the bombing referred to themselves as "Saudi Hezbollah," and they drove the truck bomb from its assembly point in the Bekáa Valley to Dhahran, Saudi Arabia.

The terrorist attack on the Khobar Towers was approved by Ayatollah Khamenei, the Supreme Leader of Iran. . . . It was also approved and supported by the Iranian Minister of Intelligence and Security (MOIS) . . . Ali Fallahian, who was involved in providing intelligence security support for the operation.

The FBI also obtained a great deal of information linking the defendants to the bombing from interviews with six admitted members of the Saudi Hezbollah organization. . . . These six individuals admitted to the FBI . . . that senior officials in the Iranian government provided them with funding, planning, training, sponsorship, and travel necessary to carry out the attack. . . . The six . . . also indicated that the selection of the target and the authorization to proceed was done collectively by Iran, MOIS, and IRGC, though the actual preparation and carrying out of the attack was done by the IRGC[18]

The entire operation was conceived, organized, and controlled by the Islamic Republic from beginning to end. The indictment of Khamenei is particularly important in light of some of the later debates about the possibility of independent action by the Revolutionary Guards. The court was quite clear that all actions by the IRGC have to be approved by the Supreme Leader, to whom they report.

While some tangential evidence suggests Al Qaeda was involved in the Khobar Towers attack, it is not definitive, while the evidence against Iran is overwhelming. In the case of the embassy bombings, evidence against both is clear. The carefully orchestrated operation, involving two huge explosions at virtually the same moment at two different locations far apart from one another, seems copied right out of the Hezbollah playbook. The Al Qaeda terrorists who carried out the operations were trained by Hezbollah, and the explosives came from Iran.[19]

---

[18] http://online.wsj.com/public/resources/documents/law_ktower-opinion.pdf.
[19] Dan Eggen, "9/11 Panel Links Al Qaeda, Iran," *Washington Post*, June 26, 2004.

The court's finding that the Iranians were up to their necks in the African embassy bombings gainsays another of the principal tenets of the U.S. intelligence community: that Iran ceased supporting terrorist operations against Americans by 1996. This reassuring bit of conventional wisdom has been endorsed by some of the most talented and intelligent analysts, such as Richard Clarke and Steven Simon, who claim that we frightened the Iranians into abandoning such efforts.[20] And Kenneth Pollack agrees, saying that there is no evidence of a direct or indirect Iranian attack since '96.[21]

And then there is the important story of Abu Musab al-Zarqawi, the Jordanian member of Al Qaeda who for a while became the deus ex machina of the terror war in Iraq. His name first became celebrated when Secretary of State Colin Powell named Zarqawi as a vital link between Iraq and Al Qaeda. As I wrote at the time,[22] the story of Zarqawi proves more than Powell intended, since there was so much evidence—indeed, a small mountain of court documents, some from Germany and others from Italy—

---

[20] Richard Clarke and Steven Simon, "Bombs That Would Backfire," *The New York Times*, April 16, 2006.

[21] Kenneth Pollack, *The Persian Puzzle* (New York: Random House, 2004) 298–99.

[22] I believe I was the first American writer to deal with Zarqawi, in *National Review Online*, December 12, 2002.

that he was in cahoots with the regime in Tehran. The information was not secret; anyone could go to the courts and read it, and the German evidence was written up in *Die Zeit* in early December 2002, recounting the case against a terrorist called Abdullah S. Thanks to his cooperation with the authorities, the Germans had rounded up a terrorist cell of thirteen Palestinians—their organization was known as al Tawhid—that had planned terrorist operations in Europe against Jews and Americans, and against German military targets.

Die Zeit was quite categorical about the basic facts: Zarqawi was the head of al Tawhid, he was simultaneously a top officer of Al Qaeda, and he lived in and worked out of Tehran. Abdullah S. insisted to German intelligence officers that al Tawhid could not function without the active support of the Iranian regime, and the Germans provided many chapters and many verses with pithy details:

• Zarqawi was a Palestinian with a Jordanian passport, and he supervised terrorist training camps near Herat and Kabul, thus confirming the ongoing role of Iran/Al Qaeda in organizing and running terrorist operations in Afghanistan.

• According to German intelligence, Zarqawi was a key figure in the "reorganized Al Qaeda," as well as one of the major coordinators of Iranian-sponsored terrorism in Europe. His group, al Tawhid, arranged false documentation for more than one hundred Al Qaeda fighters who escaped from Afghanistan during the war, provided them with funds, passports, and safe haven (near Tehran), and then organized their movement out of Iran to other areas, some in the Middle East, others—as the case of Abdullah S. demonstrated—in the West.

• Iran is a major center for Al Qaeda, and the Germans identified roughly a dozen camps around Tehran where Al Qaeda terrorists were taken care of by the Iranian Revolutionary Guards. These camps were part of an elaborate underground railroad: the terrorists and their families moved out of Afghanistan and Pakistan into Iranian Baluchistan and then into Iran proper. From there they went by air or land either to Beirut or to Damascus (the State Department's "ally" in the war against terror), and then into the Bekáa Valley of Lebanon to one of the legendary centers of Hezbollah terror, ein Hilweh. Once their training and phony identities were completed, they moved on.

• The Germans confirmed that there were meetings, ongoing cooperation, between Al Qaeda's Osama bin Laden and Hezbollah's Imad Mughniyah. They not only cooperated on terrorist operations, but also worked closely to secure their wealth: Al Qaeda and Hezbollah moved gold and diamonds from Karachi to Sudan, via Iran.

The same picture emerged from a court case in Milan, Italy, where the prosecution introduced intercepts of conversations between Zarqawi and his Italian agents and couriers. His calls—on a variety of satellite, cell, and landline telephones—demonstrated that he was in Tehran at the time. Finally, a leading Italian magistrate in Milano, Stefano Dambruoso, added some detail to the picture of Zarqawi in a book entitled *Milan-Baghdad*.

Dambruoso flatly confirms Zarqawi's Iran connection: "Our investigations permit us to establish that country of the ayatollahs is the preferred springboard for militants headed for Iraq." According to Dambruoso, Zarqawi had already organized groups of fighters before the liberation of Iraq, and they operated alongside the remnants of Saddam's killers. The European network was used to recruit new bodies for the jihad in Iraq, and they entered from Iran in groups of three to five at a time, with phony passports and usually pretending to be businessmen. They rented or bought small apartments in Baghdad, Tikrit, and Ramadi, where they organized larger cells, then moved into the battle area. Zarqawi himself entered Iraq by this method, along with one of the leading ideologues of the jihad, Abu Masaab (a Syrian).

According to a 2004 story in *Asharq Al-Awsat*, a commander of the Iranian Revolutionary Guards told the participants in a high-level meeting in Tehran that Zarqawi and twenty other senior members of the terrorist group Ansar al-Islam had free passage between Iran and Iraq. Asked why Iran would support Zarqawi, whose anti-Shi'ite diatribes and massacres were known to all, the commander calmly replied that Zarqawi's actions in Iraq "serve the supreme interests of Iran" by preventing the creation of a pro-U.S. government.

The comforting conviction that Iran had abandoned anti-American terrorism in the mid-1990s was totally wrong, and it may well have contributed to our failure to spot the conspiracy that executed the largest terrorist attack on American soil.

SEPTEMBER 11

Two big-time commissions and scores of books later, we have still not unraveled all the threads of the September 11 conspiracy. If we ever do, I suspect we will be amazed at the number of terrorist groups—and their national sponsors—that were involved in the conspiracy.

Most people have forgotten the "big news" from the 9/11 Commission, namely that its members were astonished to find various links between the Al Qaeda terrorists and the Islamic Republic. They didn't have time to look very deeply into the subject—the CIA unaccountably waited until just twenty-four hours before the report had to be delivered to the publisher before presenting commission staffers with the documents—and they contented themselves with a request that the government fully investigate the connections. If this has been done, the results are not public. But we do know enough to be able to say that it is altogether possible that the Islamic Republic was up to its neck in the operation.

- We know that in October and November 2000, Imad Mughniyah and some of his top aides personally accompanied the so-called 9/11 "muscle hijackers" out of Saudi Arabia, via Tehran and Beirut. Given Mughniyah's unique standing with the Islamic Republic, and his legendary role in the terror network, it is hard to believe this was not approved at the highest levels in Tehran.

• We know that the key intermediary between Al
Qaeda's leaders and the terrorists who flew the
planes on 9/11—Ramzi Binalshibh—acquired an
Iranian visa at the embassy in Berlin in late 2000,
and that he flew to Tehran on January 31 (a trip of
which the 9/11 Commission was apparently un-
aware). Some have speculated that, like many Al
Qaeda operatives, Binalshibh used Iran as a pas-
sageway to and from Afghanistan, where bin
Laden, Zawahiri, and the other top figures were
located.

• We know that in early September 2001, just before the attack against America, Binalshibh went to
Iran.[23]

• We know that the remnants of Al Qaeda ran from
Afghanistan into Iran, and that they reconstituted
their organization there. These are the conclusions
of the Spanish investigative magistrate Baltasar
Garzón, who has spent most of his adult life looking
into the terror network. According to Garzón, "Al
Qaeda has been restructured and has a 'board of
managers' in Iran."[24]

---

[23] John Crewdson, "As U.S. Steps Up Investigation, Iran Denies As-
sisting Al Qaeda," *Chicago Tribune*, July 21, 2004.
[24] http://english.aljazeera.net/English/archive/archive?ArchiveId=
1662.

Garzón was proven right by subsequent attacks. Less than a year later, on April 11, 2002, an Al Qaeda suicide bomber killed nineteen people in a synagogue in Tunisia. NBC News reported that the terrorist cell had been in contact with Saad bin Laden, Osama's son, from a safe haven in Iran. The Al Qaeda spokesman, Suleiman Abu Ghaith, triumphantly proclaimed Al Qaeda's credit for the massacre, also from Iran. Thirteen months afterward, on May 12, 2003, Saad bin Laden, still in Iran, ordered simultaneous attacks in Riyadh, Saudi Arabia. One of the suspects escaped to Iran.

Bob Baer, one of the most intrepid and serious CIA case officers in recent years, put it succinctly in his bestselling *See No Evil*:

Before I left the CIA in late 1997, we had learned that bin Laden had suggested to the Iranians that they drop their efforts to undermine central Asian governments and instead join him in a campaign against the United States. We knew, too, that in July 1996 bin Laden's allies . . . had been in touch with Imad Mughniyah. . . . Throw in bin Laden's connections to the Egyptian fundamentalists and what we have is the most formidable terrorist coalition in history.[25]

---

[25] Robert Baer, *See No Evil: The True Story of a Ground Soldier in the CIA's War on Terrorism* (New York: Crown, 2002), 269.

Indeed, while there is still much we do not know, it seems likely that the remnant of Al Qaeda that limped out of Afghanistan in 2002 became irrevocably tied to Iran. I was told by usually well-informed Iranians in December 2001 that bin Laden would go to Iran and "be disappeared." The Iranians know better than anyone that a "disappeared" man can exert enormous influence over the Islamic world; it is the story of the twelfth Imam, after all.

Bin Laden did indeed vanish, and his rare subsequent appearances have been virtual ones: video and, for three years as of this writing, only audio transmissions. I was told in early 2006 that he had died and was buried in Tehran. French intelligence reported his death later in the year, although it was later denied, and the American intelligence community adamantly insisted he was still alive and was somewhere between Pakistan and Afghanistan. In any event, ever since early 2006, Ayman al-Zawahiri has acted as if he were the head of Al Qaeda, and few doubt that Zawahiri is based in Iran, along with Saad bin Laden and other top members of the Al Qaeda leadership.

This means that Al Qaeda no longer exists as a separate entity, and that it has been integrated into the terrorist galaxy that revolves around Iran. Like Hezbollah, Islamic Jihad, and, increasingly, Hamas, Al Qaeda depends on Tehran for the wherewithal any terrorist organization needs to be effective: safe havens, training facilities, weapons, laboratories, false documents, access to the media for its propaganda. It is hard to imagine that Al Qaeda could do anything contrary to the wishes of the mullahs, or that it could fail to obey instructions from the Revolutionary Guards Corps, which undoubtedly oversees its daily activities and provides the bulk of its resources.

We learned in the spring of 2007 that Hezbollah only acts with the direct, detailed and specific approval of Tehran. In a April 15 interview with the Iranian Arabic-language TV station al Qawthar, Hezbollah deputy secretary-general Naim Kassem stated that suicide bombings, terrorist attacks, and even artillery barrages against Israeli civilians all receive prior approval from the ayatollahs.[26] And the same seems to apply to Al Qaeda in Iraq, as General David Petraeus made clear in considerable detail at a press conference in Washington on April 25:

Gen. Petraeus: The Iranian involvement has really become much clearer to us and brought into

---

[26] Israeli Foreign Ministry, "Behind the Headlines: Hizbullah Leader Declares: We Get Our Orders From Tehran,"April 22, 2007.

much more focus during the interrogation of the members—the heads of the Qazali network and some of the key members of that network that have been in detention now for a month or more. This is the head of the secret cell network, the extremist secret cells. They were provided substantial funding, training on Iranian soil, advanced explosive munitions and technologies as well as run-of-the-mill arms and ammunition, in some cases advice and in some cases even a degree of direction. When we captured these individuals—the initial capture, and then there have been a number of others since then—we discovered, for example, a twenty-two-page memorandum on a computer that detailed the planning, preparation, approval process and conduct of the operation that resulted in five of our soldiers being killed in Karbala. It also detailed—there are numerous documents which detailed a number of different attacks on coalition forces, and our sense is that these records were kept so that they could be handed in to whoever it is that is financing them. And there's no question, again, that Iranian financing is taking place through the Quds Force of the Iranian Republican Guards Corps. As you know, there are seven Quds Force members in detention as well. This involvement, again, we learned more about with the detention of an individual named Sheibani, who is one of the heads of the Sheibani network, which brings explosively formed projectiles into Iraq from Iran. His brother is the Iranian connection. He is—was in Iraq. And that has been the conduit that then distributes these among the extremist elements again of these secret cells and so forth . . .

Q: May I formally ask you: What is your assessment at this point? Do you believe that the central government of Iran, Ahmadinejad himself, perhaps, is, number one, aware of this, supporting it, directing it? What is the central government involvement? Could this level of activity possibly take place without the Iranian leadership knowing about it? And just as another point, do you see any involvement beyond EFPs? Are they now involved in these spectacular suicide car-bomb attacks?

Gen. Petraeus: With respect to how high does it go and, you know, what do they know and when did they know it, I honestly cannot—that is such a sensitive issue that—and that we do not—at least I do not know of anything that specifically identifies how high it goes beyond the level of the Quds Force, Commander Suleiman. Beyond that, it is very difficult to tell—we know where he is in the overall chain of command; he certainly reports to the very top—but again, nothing that would absolutely indicate, again, how high the knowledge of this actually goes. So—

Petraeus was being very careful about the extent of his knowledge, but to believe that a Quds campaign could be conducted without Khamenei's approval is as silly as the belief that a Special Forces campaign could be conducted without White House approval. No way. So when you hear "Al Qaeda," it's probably wise to think "Iran." More than anything else, Al Qaeda today is a label the mullahs can apply to any group they wish.

IRAQ AND AFGHANISTAN

The whole world knew that we would invade Iraq and defenestrate Saddam Hussein's Baathist regime; the only real questions were about the date of the invasion and the course the war would take. No one doubted the military success of Operation Iraqi Freedom. That it was the wrong war, conducted in the wrong way, was not widely understood, because most analysts focused on Iraq alone, instead of recognizing that, once we entered the Arab Middle East, we would be engaged in a regional war and would have to face enemies more fearsome than Saddam's armies.

The war in the Middle East was of necessity regional, because once Saddam was removed, the American enterprise threatened the survival of similar tyrants from the Persian Gulf to North Africa. This threat was felt most acutely among the leaders of Iran, where the regime's lack of popular support exposed it to domestic revolt. If we succeeded in advancing freedom in both Iraq to their west and Afghanistan on their eastern frontier, the mullahs could not hope to restrain the desires for freedom by the Iranian people. It was therefore certain that Iran would do everything in its power to ensure we failed in both neighboring countries.

The same applied to Iran's main strategic ally, the Baathist Republic of Syria, governed by Bashar Assad, who incautiously announced, shortly before the American attack, that it was necessary to turn Iraq into a "second Lebanon," a clear reference to the joint Iranian-Syrian strategy in the mid-1980s that had driven the United States' armed forces out of the country. The "second Lebanon," like the first, would be based on terrorist attacks like those on the French and American marine barracks and the American embassy and annex, along with hostage taking and mass demonstrations. Assad's call to action was echoed by Ali Khamenei, who proclaimed that America would sink into a quagmire, just as had occurred in Vietnam.

In the meantime, coalition forces were destroying Al Qaeda and the Taliban in Afghanistan, and the Islamic Republic sent the foreign arm of the Revolutionary Guards, the Quds Force (of which more shortly), across its eastern border to kill Americans, and to organize the escape to Iran of the bin Ladens and their top associates. The existence of Iranian-trained and sponsored terrorist units in Afghanistan was known to the American government in mid-December 2001, as a result of conversations in Rome with knowledgeable Iranians at which I was present.

The Iranians' main agent in Afghanistan was Gulbuddin Hekhmatyar, who lived in Iran for some time during the Taliban period (even though the Taliban named him a provincial governor) and maintained luxurious residences on both sides of the border. Hekhmatyar organized armed resistance, smuggled money and weapons to the remnants of the Taliban, and worked with the Revolutionary Guards to ensure that Iran would have operational bases all over the country.

They performed remarkably well, under difficult and dangerous circumstances, although the Iranians had an enormous strategic advantage: the huge and growing

Afghan reliance on Iran for its foreign commerce (relations with Pakistan are terrible). By mid-July, Zalmay Khalilzad, U.S. special envoy, and later ambassador to Afghanistan, a naturalized Afghan, remarked that the Iranians were trying to overthrow the Karzai government. He referred to the Iranians' demonstrated ability to rescue the top level of Al Qaeda and assist many of the traditional warlords so they could join in the fight against Karzai and the Americans. By December 2001, the Islamic Republic's agents had installed AM and FM radio transmitters along the Afghan border, thereby bringing Afghanistan within the mullahs' broadcast range.

By March 2003, leading Afghans, including Ismail Khan, traveled openly to Tehran to meet with the mullahs and coordinate their campaigns against the government in Kabul. This led Karzai to fire Khan as a military commander, but Khan remained governor of Herat, where he continued to collaborate with Hekhmatyar and the Iranians.

Indeed, by March 2006, the official Afghan news agency (Bakhtar) reported that more than ten Iranian officials had been arrested in Herat in the first quarter of the year, and according to a column written by a knowledgeable Afghan in early 2007, the Iranians had adopted the same tactic as in Iraq: "Iran is ready to cooperate and support any group, regardless of their religion and language, who can fight the U.S. presence."[27]

The "first Lebanon" had marked the emergence of Hezbollah as a major force in the Middle East. The mullahs' favorite terrorist instrument had grown in strength and self-confidence in the intervening twenty years and provided much of the expertise for the "insurgency" in Iraq. As before, Imad Mughniyah was the key figure and shuttled constantly back and forth between Beirut, Damascus, Tehran, and various locations inside Iraq, even before the war began. All of this was done in accordance with a strategic plan developed among the three major leaders: Khamenei, Assad, and Saddam Hussein, with the Supreme Leader clearly the major force. Saddam was destined to be overthrown, and Syria was a pygmy compared to the Islamic Republic, to whom in any case the Assad family owed its legitimacy (Khomeini having ordered the leading Syrian Shi'ite figures to endorse Hafiz al-Assad when most Shi'ites had refused to support the Alawite Assad). As if to underline his role, Mughniyah accompanied Iranian president Mahmoud Ahmadinejad to Damascus in January 2006, where he

---

[27] See Muhammad Tahir, "Iranian Involvement in Afghanistan," *Terrorism Monitor 5*, no. 1 (January 18, 2007).

met with other terrorist leaders and the Syrian military and intelligence personnel who were to support the war in Iraq.

Anyone watching the skies between the three countries in the months leading up to the invasion of Iraq would have been surprised to see the quantity of traffic, especially that between Iran and Iraq. Previously, planes flying from Tehran to Damascus tended to carry bombs, not ministers and intelligence chiefs. To put it mildly, there was no love lost between the two countries; the ferocious war of the 1980s had produced more than a million dead and a small army of disabled veterans on both sides, and such devastation is not easily overcome even with the strongest political will. But the terror masters of the Middle East are best understood as counterparts to the mafiosi portrayed in *The Godfather*: under normal circumstances, the Mafia families fight each other with no holds barred. But when the Feds come after them, the godfathers of the Barzinis, Corleones, and the others sit down around the table and agree to a war plan. The Americans were coming, and the terror masters made a war plan.

The extent of cooperation among Iraqis, Iranians, and Syrians was publicly described in the first days of 2005 by an Iraqi terrorist by the name of Moayad Ahmed Yasseen, the leader of a major terrorist organization,

Jaish Muhammad (Muhammad's Army). He was captured a couple of months before in the big battle in Fallujah, and his account was televised on Alhurra, an Arabic-language station funded by the U.S. government.[28]

According to Yasseen—who is confirmed by several other accounts—Jaish Muhammad had been organized by Saddam Hussein in advance of the American invasion of Iraq and contained several top Baathist officials. For the better part of two years, most serious newspaper reports described it as a shadowy organization whose membership was largely unknown, although some experts believed many of its officials and fighters were Sufis, even though it had a close working relationship with Abu Musab al-Zarqawi, a fanatic Sunni who had operated for many years out of Tehran. The one thing that seemed certain was that Jaish Muhammad was not Shi'ite.

Yasseen had been a colonel in Saddam's army, which made him an experienced fighter of some importance. He told Alhurra that two other former Iraqi military officers belonging to his group were sent "to Iran in April or May, where they met a number of Iranian intelligence officials." He said they also met with Iran's Supreme

---

[28] Michael Ledeen, "Circle Squared: Iran, Iraq, Syria," *National Review Online*, January 10, 2005.

Leader, Ayatollah Ali Khamenei, and were provided with money, weapons, "and, as far as I know, even car bombs" for Jaish Muhammad.

After the liberation of Iraq in the spring of 2003, Yasseen was instructed by Saddam himself to cross into Syria and meet with a Syrian intelligence officer who would provide Jaish Muhammad with money and weapons.

Thus, a high-ranking member of the Iraqi "insurgency" worked closely with Iran and Syria, under direct orders from Saddam himself.[29]

Yasseen was a chieftain, which gave him the necessary authority to meet with the top Syrians and Iranians. Most other terrorists were simply told what to do by the hundreds (perhaps thousands) of Iranian and Syrian intelligence officers who operated inside Iraq. Some came from the Intelligence Ministry (MOIS), but most were officers in the Revolutionary Guards Corps, or from its most lethal element, the Quds (Jerusalem) Force. This special operations unit was created in the later years of the Iran-Iraq War, and today their headquarters are significantly located in the former American embassy in Tehran, a tribute to their power and importance. From the beginning, they have coordinated their work carefully with the

---

[29] Ibid.

Special Unit of the MOIS, sharing information and resources according to need. Quds now holds primary responsibility for foreign operations, as well as other special tasks (managing the Kurds, for example), a role they fulfilled in 1989, when they assassinated the Kurdish leader Abdul Rahman Ghassemlou in Vienna based on intelligence collected by the Information Ministry's spies in Austria.

Over time, Quds became a highly independent force, despite constant protests from the regular military. Its first commander was General Ahmad Vahidi (aka Chehelcheraghi), who was deputy chief of intelligence to the army chief of staff. He is now deputy to Mohsen Rezai in the National Security and Foreign Affairs Council of the Council of Experts. Given its high prestige and power, it is not surprising that the Quds Force has a virtually unlimited budget, much of which comes from profits from army engineering projects. Quds does not use banks, since all its funds are in cash. It has full logistical support from the armed forces and can directly purchase foreign weapons. One of its preferred methods is to buy Russian weapons through Belarus, where it has a considerable presence.

Its power extends to the diplomatic corps as well; it designated the Iranian ambassador to Iraq, Hassan Kazemi Qomi, who is the deputy to Quds commander

Sardar Qasim Suleimani. In late February 2003, while attending the Salahuddin (Iraqi Kurdistan) conference, the U.S. ambassador to Iraq, Zalmay Khalilzad, was overheard telling an Iraqi opposition leader that Suleimani had recently tried to kill him in Afghanistan. As Khalilzad discovered, Iranian diplomats are dangerous people. Indeed, virtually the entire "diplomatic staff" in Iraq comes from the officer corps of the Quds Force.

The top level of Quds speaks volumes about its power, from its commander in chief, Brigadier General Qasim Suleimani, to his deputy (and simultaneously ambassador to Iraq) Brigadier General Kazemi Qomi, and the next ranking officer, Brigadier General Jafari, the man who oversaw the assassination of Ghassemlou in Vienna. These men manage the Iranian terror war in Iraq, in close coordination with their counterparts in Syria, and under the direct supervision of the Supreme Leader, to whom Suleimani reports personally. The war in Iraq is only part of their global portfolio. As the best short analysis of Quds' role in the Iranian terror network aptly summarized the available information, "under Suleimani—and his predecessor Ahmad Vahidi—Quds Force has been linked to nearly every instance of Iranian-backed terrorism over the course of the last decade." The claim was based on what the *Washington Post* called "a U.S.

intelligence analysis" that presented a fairly detailed picture of many of Quds' activities.[30] And that picture was very much at odds with the conventional wisdom, especially that regarding the possibility of Sunni/Shi'ite cooperation:

> Quds Force has agents in most countries with large Muslim populations and its goal is to "form relationships with Islamic militant and radical groups and offer financial support either to the groups at large or to Islamic figures within them who are sympathetic to the principles and foreign policy goals of the Iranian government." The analysis also stated that Quds Force had trained more than three dozen Shi'ite and Sunni foreign Islamic militant groups in paramilitary, guerrilla, and terror tactics, including assassination, kidnapping, torture, and explosives.[31]

Any group willing to kill infidels was worthy of Iranian support, in both Iraq and Afghanistan. Similar information was printed in the British press as well: Con Coughlin wrote in *The Daily Telegraph* in early 2006 that

---

[30] Dana Priest and Douglas Farah, "Iranian Force Has Long Ties to Al Qaeda," *The Washington Post*, October 14, 2003.
[31] Dan Darling, "General Panic; Meet Brigadier General Qasim Suleimani, the Commander of Iran's Anti-American Quds Force," *The Weekly Standard*, October 5, 2005.

the IRGC was "training hundreds of Al Qaeda fighters to carry out attacks against coalition forces throughout the Middle East."[32] And the foot soldiers crossed the border into Iraq by the thousands, disguised as students, pilgrims, businessmen, and even tourists (ostensibly headed for Syria, a popular vacation spot for Iranians).

The Quds Force and the MOIS jointly managed the "second Lebanon," and the foot soldiers were provided by a variety of militias, usually associated with a particular Shi'ite leader. The Iranians had patiently prepared for this moment for a long time. During the Iran-Iraq War in the 1980s, millions of Iraqi Shi'ites had gone over to the Iranian side, and they and their children had lived in Iran ever since.[33] Once it became clear that Saddam was going to be destroyed, the Iranians organized those refugees into armies capable of dominating the new Iraq. The most important of those armies were the Badr Brigades (the military wing of SCIRI, the Supreme Council for Islamic

---

[32] Con Coughlin, "Iranians Training Qaeda Terrorists to Attack Our GIs," *The Daily Telegraph*, November 14, 2006.

[33] This raises an interesting question of analysis: how do you define those millions of people, and above all, their children? Are they Iraqis (but they have lived in Iran for a generation)? Are they Iranians (but they fled an Iraqi regime and still have strong feelings of identification with Iraq)? That is why the many definitions of "the insurgency," according to which most "insurgents" are "Iraqis," are extremely misleading. Most of them are under Iranian guidance and/or control.

Revolution in Iraq), more than ten thousand strong. SCIRI's historic leader, the Ayatollah Muhammad Baqr al-Hakim, returned to Iraq from Iran in May 2003 and immediately demonstrated considerable independence from his Iranian taskmasters and supported the temporary Governing Council created by the United States. He was blown up in August, along with a hundred other victims, in Najaf. He was succeeded by his brother, Abdel Aziz, who has predictably been more responsive to the mullahs' desires. As of the summer of 2004, "Iran was paying the salaries of at least 11,740 members of the Badr Corps," according to British and American intelligence officers.[34]

The militia leader best known to Americans is Moqtada Sadr, the son of Muhammad Sadeq Sadr, an enormously popular Iraqi Shi'ite cleric who was murdered by Saddam's agents in 1999. Moqtada was virtually unknown outside Iraq before the U.S.-led invasion in March 2003, but was spotted by the Quds leaders and brought to prominence by dint of Iranian support. Moqtada inherited control of his father's vast network of charitable institutions and used it as a political power base, on which he organized his Mahdi Army.

---

[34] Michael Ware, "Inside Iran's Secret War for Iraq," *Time*, August 14, 2005.

As Michael Rubin ironically noted, "Despite allegedly representing the most impoverished fringe of Iraqi society, Mr. al-Sadr nevertheless manages to finance transport and meals for those making the weekly six-hour round-trip between Baghdad and Kufa to hear him read sermons."[35] The money comes from Iran, via Ayatollah Kazem al-Haeri, a close friend and ally of Supreme Leader Khamenei's. According to an April 8, 2004, report in the Italian daily *La Stampa*, the Italian military intelligence agency, SISMI, concluded that Iran's Supreme Leader sent Ayatollah al-Haeri to manage the campaign to drive the coalition out of Iraq. That account is almost certainly wrong; an enterprise of such dimensions was undoubtedly entrusted to the professionals in the Quds Force and their Hezbollah allies. At most, Haeri was stage-managed as Moqtada's spiritual adviser (trying to give some religious legitimacy to a man who was too young and uncultured to inspire the faithful on his own) and banker. SISMI estimated that the Quds Force was spending $70 million a month to support Moqtada and a few other favorites.

La Stampa also reported that Iran had rented two thousand seven hundred apartments for Quds Force

---

[35] Michael Rubin, "The Puppetmasters," *The New York Sun*, April 12, 2004.

agents serving in Najaf and Karbala and also ran a network of three hundred agents posing as Iranian television and print journalists who helped organize Mr. al-Sadr's operations in southern Iraq.

Moqtada's subservience to Iran was clear from the outset. In late 2003 he went to Tehran to meet with General Suleimani, who set up training camps for the Mahdi Army along the Iran/Iraq border. The Quds Force also kicked in $80 million to Moqtada for his political and military enterprises. Thereafter, whenever he needed help or advice (or whenever the mullahs got annoyed with his excesses, which was not uncommon), he would repair to Iran. The most recent such example was late 2006–early 2007, when he repaired to Tehran as the new American "surge" strategy was announced, and the Iraqi government approved stern action against Moqtada's stronghold in Sadr City, a poor neighborhood in Baghdad.

At least for a while, Moqtada was an important element in Iran's primary strategic objective in Iraq, which was to throw the country into chaos by supporting both sides in every imaginable religious and ethnic conflict. Chief among these was Sunni against Shi'ite, but the Iranians also sponsored Kurds against Arabs (and vice versa), and tribe against tribe. But Moqtada was only one element. *Time*'s man in Baghdad, Michael Ware, provided good perspective on the coordinated Iranian operation a couple of years ago: "The various groups were organized under the command of Brigadier General Qasim Suleimani . . . the exile militias brought . . . forbidding religious strictures. 'These guys with beards and Kalashnikovs showed up saying they'd come to protect the campus,' says a student leader at a Basra university. 'The problem is, they never left.' . . . 'From the beginning, the Islamic parties filled the void,' says a police lieutenant colonel. . . . 'You can't do anything without them.'"[36]

It was a replay of Hezbollah's methods in Lebanon. Brutal imposition of Sharia law went hand in hand with social welfare, and "aid" to schools, which soon became recruiting centers for the jihad. Unlike coalition forces, which moved rapidly from city to city to destroy Saddam's regime, the Iranian agents came and stayed, gaining an enormous degree of control throughout the country. It was hard for coalition officers to see what was going on, because so many members of the invading Quds Force were originally Iraqis.

A model available for us to understand Iran's methods in Iraq is the penetration and domination of the Palestinian terrorist organizations during the first

---

[36] Ware, "Inside Iran's Secret War."

intifada. The Israelis had learned a great deal about the Iranians' methods, which were replicated in Iraq a few years later. One of their most successful techniques was to use ostensibly humanitarian organizations to recruit their agents. During the intifada, for example, hundreds of injured Palestinians were taken directly to Iran for medical treatment, and during their stay in specially organized hospitals, the Palestinians were recruited by the Quds Force. As the Israelis reported, "This activity includes gathering intelligence information . . . recruiting an infrastructure of facilitators for carrying out terrorist activities, and smuggling weapons under the guise of business. . . . A portion of the wounded underwent military training during their stay in Iran; others were recruited to locate other Palestinians for carrying out military activities."[37] The wounded Palestinians received medical treatment and a stipend and were given "activist" cover. Some of them were sent to various Iranian universities to participate in local elections, thus learning political techniques as well as espionage and terrorism.

The recruitment was not left in the hands of low-level

---

[37] Israeli Ministry of Foreign Affairs, "Iranian Activities in Support of the Palestinian Intifada," January 30, 2003, http://www.mfa.gov.il/ MFA/MFAArchive/20000-2009/2003/1/Iranian%20activities%20in %20support%of%20the%Palestinian%20i.

officers; their hospital wards were visited by some of the most important figures in Iran and indeed in the region, including Hezbollah chief Hassan Nasrallah, the director general of President Khatami's office, the speaker of the Iranian parliament, high-ranking Hamas representatives from Lebanon, Iran, and the territories, the leader of the Palestinian Islamic Jihad and "Abu Jihad," a top Islamic Jihad leader in Iran.

In a pattern that was repeated in Iraq, the Iranians were particularly interested in Palestinians with expertise in chemistry and electricity, who were then trained to build explosive devices. And for those Palestinians who were selected to lead armed groups, there was plenty of money available, and professional "cover" for their activities. One "Jihad Basha," for example, received $30,000 to set up a five-man terrorist squad whose activities would be hidden within a construction company.

The Iranian war plan in Iraq, as in Israel, required a lot of money and tens of thousands of foot soldiers, and the regime had plenty of each at its disposal, along with its legendary cunning, patience, and brutality. The Iranians' lofty ambitions did not stop them from conducting a wide-scale campaign of revenge against Iraqis who had participated in the Iran-Iraq War. "According to an ex–Iraqi air force pilot . . . when the coalition forces were busy fighting the insurgency and preparing for the first national elections, the Iranian militias were busy assassinating over ninety air force pilots and other high-ranking military officers that had participated in the Iran-Iraq War."[38]

It is often said that the Iranians wish to keep their actions hidden, preferring stealth to an open campaign. But this is only true in part; they certainly act secretly in Iraq, Afghanistan, and against Israel, because their enemies are in control of the territory and can win any pitched battle. In Lebanon, where Hezbollah controls a lot of territory, and where Syrian military might looms on the border, the mullahs act more openly (although their agents, such as Mughniyah, only move in the shadows). Hezbollah cheerfully boasts that it receives an enormous amount of aid from Iran, and the mullahs proudly confirm it. Nobody in Lebanon doubts it. Sa'ad Hariri, the son of the assassinated prime minister, Rafiq Hariri, told an interviewer in early January 2007, "An executive order came from outside, and the Hezbollah leadership and Syria's allies in Lebanon are seeking to implement the orders from Syria and

---

[38] Mohammed Ayach Alkabessee, "The Iranian Role in Iraq After the Occupation," March 18, 2006, http://www.iraq-amsi.org.

Iran."[39] Those orders—to Hezbollah—are to over-throw the democratically elected government as soon as possible and reduce Lebanon once again to a Syrian/Iranian puppet state.

THE NUCLEAR QUESTION

Western diplomacy has run around in a closed circle for several years in a patently fatuous effort to negotiate an end to Iran's secret nuclear program. No serious person can possibly believe that negotiations—nor, in all likelihood, mild economic sanctions—will compel the mullahs to end the enrichment of uranium. Nor can any serious person believe that Iran's ambitions are limited to the construction of nuclear plants for the production of electricity. If that were all the mullahs wanted, they could have done the whole thing openly, with the full approval and assistance of the many countries that have mastered this technology. They did not, preferring clandestine laboratories, underground facilities, tunnels carved into the sides of mountains, secret heavy-water programs, and

---

[39] MEMRI, "Sa'ad Al-Hariri: 'Iran Is Playing a Dangerous Role in Lebanon,'" Special Dispatch Series no. 1419, January 11, 2007.

secret collusion with the archcriminals of the nuclear market: North Korea, Libya, Belarus, China, and Pakistan's infamous Dr. A. Q. Khan.

The genesis of this secret program is well-known: in 1991, at a meeting of the Iranian National Security Council, considerable attention was devoted to the humiliating retreat imposed on Saddam Hussein in Kuwait. The Iranian strategists reasoned that if Saddam had possessed nuclear weapons, the Americans and their allies would not have dared to attack, and Saddam would have kept Kuwait. Since the Iranians did not wish to be humiliated by the Americans, the Islamic Republic would have to develop her own nuclear weapons. Their program is thus some sixteen years old, four times as long as it took the United States to develop the first atomic bomb during the Second World War.

The American intelligence community does not believe Iran is on the verge of being able to test, let alone deploy, atomic bombs. The 2005 National Intelligence Estimate (NIE) flatly stated that Iran was ten years away from obtaining (wihtery) nuclear technology. But our intelligence experts have a bad track record on predicting when foreign countries would go nuclear. We were surprised in almost every case, from the Soviet Union and China to Pakistan and India. The Iranians have every incentive to hide the truth from us, and they excel at deception. What is publicly known, furthermore, shows the Iranians are going all out to bring their program to completion as quickly as they can. At the same time, they are spending an extraordinary amount of money and manpower to protect the program against attack.

As far back as 1995, the Iranians were obtaining fissionable material from Russia and the other countries of the Commonwealth of Independent States (CIS). "Between 665 and 2,000 grams of weapon-grade uranium were stolen from Georgia's Sukhumi nuclear research center around 1995, when a gruesome ethnic conflict took place there, and groups of Chechen gunmen came to support one of the sides . . . the trail of several local experts who left the Sukhumi center in that period led to Tehran. These experts specialized in designing gas centrifuges for uranium enrichment."[40]

The collapse of the Soviet Union had put considerable numbers of nuclear physicists on the streets, and Iran was happy to hire them. Georgian president Eduard Shevardnadze asked rhetorically at a press conference why nobody seemed concerned at the exodus of his country's top

---

[40] Ze'ev Wolfson, "The Moscow-Tehran-Damascus Axis Under Construction: Nuclear, Terror and Anti-Terror Interests," *Nativ on Line* 8 (October 2005).

nuclear scientists to Tehran, and that was only one case among many; in the early nineties "dozens, if not hundreds, of Russian and Ukrainian specialists left, mostly covertly, their home countries to work in Iran on 'physics' research."[41]

In its weekend edition of November 10, 2006, the Israeli Hebrew-language newspaper *Yedi'ot Aharonot* published a special supplement on the Iranian nuclear project. The supplement contained current satellite photographs that showed "extensive construction work" at a main centrifuge site, "including tunnels and bunkers," rapid progress under way at the heavy-water project, "production of UF6 gas in Isfahan which, according to intelligence reports, is supposed to be enough for two atomic bombs," and hints that the Iranians were testing explosives that could be used to trigger nuclear fission.

The satellite data came from the Ikonos (commercial) satellite, which can accurately identify objects one meter or larger. The photographs also showed that antiaircraft missile batteries were being deployed around the sites—twenty-six "antiaircraft positions" at Natanz alone—and

---

[41] Dany Shoham and Stuart M. Jacobsen, "Technical Intelligence in Retrospect: The 2001 Anthrax Letters Powder," *International Journal of Intelligence and Counterintelligence* 20 (2007): 79–105.

also a network of underground tunnels, the creation of which had thrown up an enormous quantity of earth. The newspaper repeated earlier suggestions that Iranian nuclear scientists had been present at the recent (failed) nuclear test in North Korea and noted that UN inspectors had repeatedly been denied access to one of the principal sites.

It was no accident that an Israeli newspaper devoted so much space to this subject; every major Iranian leader, from Khomeini to Khamenei, including the "moderate" Khatami, has called for the destruction of Israel, and former president Hashemi Rafsanjani publicly mused that it would be a bargain for Iran to nuke Israel, even if the Israelis responded in kind. President Ahmadinejad has openly forecast "a world without Israel" and promised that the day of Israel's destruction would soon arrive.

THE FUTURE OF THE IRANIAN WAR PLAN

As the mullahs surveyed the battlefields in early 2007, they had many reasons for optimism. The biggest strategic development was the sudden rise to power of the Democratic Party in the United States, whose leaders seemed determined to withdraw American troops from

Iraq as quickly as possible. If that were to take place, the Islamic Republic would be the dominant force in Iraq, and thus in the entire region. If, at the same time, the nuclear program came to fruition—and the Western countries showed no sign of taking effective action to prevent it—the mullahs could well expect to impose an Islamic republic on Iraq, topple the free government in Lebanon, and solidify their alliance with Syria. From this imposing strategic base, Iran could then concentrate its considerable strength on the destruction of Israel, and the downfall of the United States.

By early 2007, the mullahs were convinced that the United States was on the same death spiral as the Soviet Union had navigated a quarter century earlier, and for the same reason: its will had been broken in a conflict with superior Islamic forces. Khamenei and his cohorts believed the Soviet Union had been defeated by Islam in Afghanistan and therefore collapsed. Once America, the twentieth century's other superpower, was defeated by Islam in Iraq, it would fall into the same grave as its historical adversary.

"The Americans have many weaknesses," RG commander Yahya Rahim Safavi proclaimed on Iranian television. "We have planned our strategy precisely on the basis of their strengths and weaknesses." These weaknesses are, above all, human: "When their commanders encounter a problem, they burst into tears. We did not see such spectacles in the eight years of the Iran-Iraq War."[42] To be sure, this is propaganda, primarily designed to convince the Iranian people that the United States is impotent against the regime's brilliance and cunning. But there is more to it than that; these are messianics who believe their moment of glory has come and is favored by divine forces. The symbol of this messianic cult is President Mahmoud Ahmadinejad, a member of the Hojatieh cult, which is dedicated to do everything possible to hasten the return of the Mahdi, and thus the end of the world. Khomeini—Khomeini!—had banned the group, which he considered too extreme. But it now has revived standing. Ahmadinejad and his cohorts have "propelled the regime's revolution toward a cataclysmic confrontation with the West." The distinguished and prolific writer and editor, Amir Taheri says, "The real crisis is much broader than nuclear weapons; it's about Iran's determination to reshape the Middle East . . . a deliberate clash of civilizations with the United States."

On the other hand, the war in Iraq had not gone as well as the mullahs had hoped. Despite enormous human and financial resources at their disposal (and a welcome

---

[42] MEMRI Special Dispatch—Iran, November 17, 2006, www.memritv.org/search.asp?ACT=S9&P1=1318.

increase in the price of oil, thereby giving them even more money to play with), and an intimate knowledge of the country, there was still nothing approaching the sort of mass anticoalition uprising the Iranians had tried to provoke. Nor had the violent ethnic conflict erupted into a national civil war. Indeed, there were bothersome signs that significant blocs of the Iraqi population were prepared to challenge Iranian- and Syrian-supported terrorist groups—such as "Al Qaeda in Iraq"—on the ground and even fight alongside coalition troops in places like Anbar Province, where terrorists crossing the Iraq/Syria border had previously had a relatively free run.

In addition, the Iranian forces in Iraq showed a worrisome tendency to go over to the other side. The most dramatic case was the disappearance of the former deputy defense minister General Ali Reza Asgari from Istanbul in early March 2007. The Iranians immediately announced that he had been kidnapped by the Americans and/or the Israelis, although the possibility of his defection remained open. Either way, it was a major loss to the regime, since he was generally considered one of the men who had created Hezbollah and would know a great deal about the organization's activities in Iraq. *Asharq Al-Awsat* reported around the same time that dozens of RG members and military intelligence operatives in Iraq had defected to the United States over the past three years.[43]

But even if the auguries were overwhelmingly negative, the leaders of the Islamic Republic would continue to wage its unholy war against us, as it had for twenty-eight years. The question for the United States was not whether war with Iran was inevitable; it was already raging. The question was whether the United States was prepared to fight back effectively, and on the full battlefield.

---

[43] *Ynetnews.com*, March 14, 2007.

3   THE AMERICAN RESPONSE

America can not do a damn thing.

    —Ayatollah Khomeini, following the hostage seizure, 1979

There has been no break in ideological or operational continuity from Khomeini to Khamenei and Ahmadinejad; only the public face of the Revolution has changed. America was proclaimed the Great Satan in 1979, and the Great Satan it remains. The destruction of Israel was invoked in 1979 and is promised every week. Iran created, supported, and penetrated the major terrorist organizations and still does today. The Iranian war against the United States was announced even before Khomeini became the Supreme Leader of an Islamic fascist theocracy, and Iran has waged that war uninterruptedly.

In like manner, the American response (or rather, the lack of an appropriately forceful American response) has remained constant for nearly three decades: a triumph of hope over all available evidence, an insistence that, no matter how bad things look, patient diplomacy will eventually yield a "solution," and that the Iranian regime, like all regimes, is interested in advancing the interests of the state and would therefore be amenable to reason combined with moderate pressure.

Alongside the failure to respond to Iran's numerous acts of war against the United States goes the ongoing failure of the intelligence community to see what is actually going on in Iran. This, too, goes back to the genesis of the Khomeini regime. At that time, the CIA failed to understand the two key figures in the run-up to the Islamic Revolution: Khomeini and the shah. The Agency did not know the shah was dying of cancer and, in any case, mistakenly thought he was a tough leader who would fiercely fight to retain his throne. The CIA did not recognize the true nature of the ayatollah's worldview and did not think he was capable of leading a revolution.

In part, this failure could be explained by the turmoil that had roiled the Agency after the scandals of the late sixties and early seventies, widely publicized in public hearings by Senate and House committees. A crucial number of experienced case officers were driven into early retirement, and their successors were gun-shy. The CIA would routinely have recruited agents inside the opposition in the past, but they did not do so in Iran and consequently lacked good sources at the moment of truth.

Several other factors blinded the intelligence community to the nature of Khomeini's movement, ranging from a crucial shortage of Farsi speakers (most of the analysts working on Iran were Arabists and had spent most of their careers in the Arab-speaking states of the Gulf and North Africa), to wrongheaded social-science models of revolution that made it impossible to recognize the dynamism of the clerical fascism that would soon sweep away the shah. When the CIA created an emergency task force on Iran in December 1978, its head came from the Arab States Branch. Meanwhile, the CIA station chief in Tehran had just arrived from Tokyo, having spent his career in the Orient, without any significant knowledge of the Middle East.

Even those who recognized that Iran was in the throes of a revolutionary upheaval believed that the opposition was basically secular and essentially democratic. It was next to impossible to find anyone in the intelligence community, or for that matter in the foreign service, or among their friends and consultants in academia, who strongly disagreed with the notion that Khomeini was little more than a somewhat eccentric but profoundly religious figure, a view encapsulated in Andrew Young's famous remark that the ayatollah was "some kind of a saint."

Two American allies—France and Israel—foresaw the coming crisis and recognized the terrible consequences that would follow a seizure of power by Khomeini's movement. Both countries shared their assessment with the Americans, who thought it was garbage.

The nature of politics being local and personal, each successive administration's failure has been blamed on the shortcomings of one leader or another, or on the particular ideological bent of the president. This must be wrong; such impressive continuity points to much deeper causes, lodged in American character.

In the face of centuries of violent human history that indicate the contrary, Americans are the first people in the history of the world to believe that peace is the normal condition of mankind. This quaint article of faith blends nicely with two other American conceits, that all people are equally good, and all problems can be solved, if only one has enough patience and goodwill. In recent years, the dangerous doctrines of political correctness and multiculturalism have added another subtheme: the notion that all cultures and practices are entitled to the same respect because, in the end, there is no truly objective standard. It follows that we should strive for "understanding," the better to achieve harmonious relations with one and all. Rare indeed is the American leader who believes that we have real enemies, with whom no modus vivendi can be reached, because those enemies truly desire our destruction or domination, as is the case with the mullahs.

These beliefs have shaped the behavior of every American president since Jimmy Carter, and the mullahs have carefully exploited them. The pattern was evident in the days immediately following the Islamic Revolution, when the Carter administration, having convinced itself that "we could live with" the Ayatollah Khomeini's new regime in Iran, strove mightily to demonstrate our goodwill and willingness to find common ground.

Khomeini's fundamentalism did not exclude the acquisition of modern weapons, and Iran's appetite for advanced American military technology remained a constant theme in the years ahead. As soon as the shah's regime had fallen, the country's new military leaders pressed the United States for matériel, from spare parts for artillery and transport vehicles, and above all for the air force, which was composed mostly of American fighter planes and helicopter warships. The Carter administration's representatives, whether in Tehran or Washington, were happy to comply, provided that everything be promptly paid for. Ironically, the Iranians' first attempts to buy American weaponry were sabotaged by their own fanatics; just as had happened in the latter days of the shah, employees at the Central Bank of Iran blocked any checks to an American entity.

The Americans were so eager to consummate the sales—which the State Department and Pentagon viewed as a way to build goodwill between the two countries— that they came up with the diplomatic equivalent of a Rube Goldberg device. Most American citizens had fled Iran quite suddenly during the Revolution, but many of their personal effects had stayed behind. This situation offered the makings of a clever deal: the Iranian regime was hired to fly these things—mostly household furniture and the like—to the United States. A credit was temporarily issued to Iran for services rendered, then recycled back to the American government for the purchase of weapons, which were then loaded onto the same transport planes that had carried the Americans' property.

It wasn't nearly good enough for the new Iranian regime. With all the goodwill in the world, the Americans couldn't generate enough credits for furniture shipments to satisfy the mullahs' appetites, which were considerable. They were planning a major military campaign against the Kurds and wanted big quantities of lethal equipment. A Pentagon team was duly dispatched to Tehran and was delighted to inform Washington that the Iranian defense minister, General Riahi, had asked the Americans to speed up the process. The White House was appropriately encouraged and, dreaming of a diplomatic breakthrough that would normalize relations with Tehran, instructed the Defense Department to act quickly. The weapons spigot was opened, and full-scale diplomatic negotiations followed almost immediately.

In what was to become the great leitmotif of American efforts to strike a "grand bargain" with the mullahs from 1979 to the present, Washington diplomats refused to see the Iranians for what they were: committed enemies of the West, cannily exploiting the Americans' desire for an agreement at all costs. The first negotiation was described in language that could well describe similar talks in Baghdad in the spring of 2007: "The air was thick with suspicion [but] there was little acrimony. The U.S. side was extraordinarily patient and understanding, repeatedly indicating willingness to review issues on their merits and to provide additional information where feasible."[1]

This led to an even higher-level meeting a couple of days later, involving Secretary of State Cyrus Vance and Khomeini's personal adviser (formally, Deputy Prime Minister for Revolutionary Affairs) Ibrahim Yazdi, who kicked off the talks by denouncing the United States for failure to accept the Revolution. Vance denied it and

---

[1] Quoted in Michael Ledeen and William Lewis, *Debacle* (New York: Knopf, 1981), 226.

pointed to several gestures that showed American acceptance. But Yazdi marched forward: the United States had
to hand over the many Iranian "criminals" who had escaped the ayatollahs' revenge and taken refuge in America; the United States must honor all the arms deals
agreed with the shah; and Carter and his people had to
remain silent about the contentious issue of human
rights, a mainstay of the administration's rhetoric and a
crucial element in the American abandonment of the
shah himself. Despite the mounting evidence of major
bloodletting in Iran, Yazdi insisted that Khomeini had led
"the cleanest revolution in world history."

Instead of coming to grips with the unpleasant reality,
the American diplomats strained to be understanding.
The assistant secretary of state for the region, Harold
Newsom, felt (as reported in the State Department cable
describing the meeting) that "the Iranian suspicions of us
were only natural in the postrevolutionary situation but
that after a transition period common interests could
provide a basis for future cooperation—'not on the scale
of before but sufficient to demonstrate that Iran has not
been "lost" to us and to the West.'"

This was written almost precisely a month before the
American embassy in Tehran was seized by what Khomeini
called the "dear students" of the Revolution. Despite the
disquieting vibes at the New York meetings, American mil-

itary officials continued to negotiate the sale of spare parts for the Iranians to use against the Kurds. The Iranians were urged to set up a major purchasing mission in Washington, thereby saving time and endless hours on intercontinental jets. While this was taken under advisement in Tehran, the State Department's Iran desk officer, Henry Precht, flew to Tehran, apparently to push hard for the Iranians to get the relationship back on track. But the Iranians were not interested in good relations. Two weeks later the embassy was stormed, putting an end to these happy thoughts, at least for the remainder of Jimmy Carter's presidency.

Before the release of the hostages was finally arranged, some 444 days later, American diplomats and various back channels put in hundreds of hours negotiating with the mullahs. In the end, Carter approved a series of humiliating concessions to get the hostages back. The day before he left office, the president signed a series of executive orders to implement his concessions to the mullahs, of which one has long stuck in the craws of the returned hostages. According to Executive Order 12283, nobody subject to American law can sue the Islamic Republic for the destruction of the Tehran embassy or for the seizure, beating, and psychological torture of the hostages.

The Carter debacle was best demonstrated in a single incident in 1979. Knowing that the Saudis were terrified by the emergence of the Islamic Republic, we sent a squadron of fighter planes to the kingdom, hoping to reassure the royal family. But Carter did not want to do anything that would unduly agitate the mullahs, and therefore the planes were unarmed. This produced a double whammy: the Saudis were disgusted and the Iranians more convinced than ever that the United States was not serious.[2]

We have been negotiating with them ever since. In the intervening twenty-eight years, we have participated in countless face-to-face encounters, myriad "démarches" sent through diplomatic channels, and meetings—some on the fringes of international conferences—involving "unofficial" representatives of one government or the other, including businessmen, journalists, and others.

But the Iranians continue to wage war against us.

REAGAN

Less than five years after the return of the embassy hostages—in the summer and fall of 1985—we were once again engaged in talks with Iran, and once again hostages were at the center of the negotiations. Despite

---

[2] Kenneth Pollack, *The Persian Puzzle* (New York: Random House, 2004), 284.

the tall tales of an "October surprise," according to which Ronald Reagan's campaign manager and later CIA chief, William Casey, developed secret channels to the mullahs and arranged to delay the hostage release until after the November 1980 elections, there were no such contacts. Had they existed, there would have been no need for the various intermediaries used in what became known as the Iran-Contra Affair.[3]

Iran-Contra was very different from the hostage negotiations in the Carter years. Carter had to deal with a full-blown international crisis created by the capture of American embassy personnel in Tehran. Reagan, too, was concerned about the several American hostages in Iranian hands, but with the exception of CIA officer William Buckley, they were private citizens, ranging from journalists and priests to academics seized from their posts at the American University in Beirut. There was no compelling policy or national security requirement that the United States deal with Iran on behalf of those unfortunates, but, as Casey's successor at CIA wrote afterward, "Reagan was motivated to go forward with the

---

[3] For the details of Iran-Contra see Michael A. Ledeen, *Perilous Statecraft: An Insider's Account of the Iran-Contra Affair* (New York: Scribner, 1989).

Iranian affair almost entirely because of his obsession with getting the American hostages freed."[4] Hostages also drove the other main player in the affair: like Reagan, Israeli prime minister Menachem Begin was similarly obsessed with the fate of his own citizens in Iranian hands. The deals with the Iranians involved all three countries; Israeli representatives were present at the talks, and many of the weapons sold to Tehran came from the Israeli inventory.

Reagan's deep personal concerns about the fate of the hostages drove our policy and inverted the logical strategic order. Iran was a major problem for the United States and should have been dealt with on that basis. The hostages were only one among many contentious issues, and far less urgent than many others, such as Iran's support for terrorism. Yet once the president insisted—over the heated objections of Secretary of State Shultz and Secretary of Defense Weinberger—that the liberation of the hostages was the number one goal, it was inevitable that the United States, as Iranian intermediary Manucher Ghorbanifar accurately put it, would become hostage to the hostages.

To make things worse, Iran policy was unexpectedly linked to the administration's search for financial support

---

[4] Robert M. Gates, *From the Shadows* (New York: Simon & Schuster, 1996), 397.

for the Nicaraguan Contras, whom we had created and then supported in their war with the Sandinistas. Congress was constantly trying to cut off their U.S. government funding, and Lieutenant Colonel Oliver North of the National Security Council staff was tasked with finding independent financial sources. North was also involved in the Iranian affair and realized that profits from arms sales to the mullahs could be routed to the Contras. As Talleyrand once remarked about one of Napoléon's schemes, it was worse than a crime, it was a blunder. It encouraged bad policy toward Iran—the weapons sales—because it helped solve a totally unrelated problem.

Thus, just as in 1979, the Islamic Republic's desire for weapons became a central theme, and for good reason: the Iran-Iraq War was raging, and the Iranians desperately wanted effective antitank missiles to counter Saddam's main advantage against them. They demanded TOW missiles and offered to obtain the release of hostages (predictably, at no time did the Iranians ever admit any responsibility for kidnapping Americans). Although a betrayal of Reagan's own announced policy of not negotiating with or making concessions to terrorists, he authorized a series of weapons sales, and provision of military intelligence about Iraq.

Some of the American officials involved in the affair convinced themselves that there was a strategic pony somewhere under the manure of the arms-for-hostages trades: the creation of privileged channels to leading Iranian "moderates" who wanted better relations with the United States. This article of faith would become even more damaging during the Clinton presidency, but it was bad enough during Reagan's second term. There was a small element of truth in the belief in "moderates" (or "pragmatists"); the Iranian regime was not totally monolithic—several factions were engaged in nasty squabbles with each other—and some of the leading mullahs did indeed want better relations with the United States. But no one in a high position in the Iranian regime was a "moderate" (there was never any convincing proof that any of our interlocutors really wanted to change the nature of the regime), and normalizing or even improving relations would have undermined any chance for fundamental change, since it would have demonstrated American acceptance of the Islamic Republic as it was. These considerations were discarded in favor of a secret diplomatic initiative: a group led by former national security adviser Robert McFarlane flew secretly to Tehran, met with a few midlevel Iranians, and returned empty-handed.

Perhaps providentially, the entire scheme was wrecked when a Lebanese newspaper published an account of the misguided enterprise, the American media soon caught up, congressional hearings were quickly organized, and the Iranian affair was totally shut down. Its positive results were meager, save for the successful ransom of a few hostages (the French and British governments ransomed their hostages at about the same time, on occasion using the same intermediary as the United States had). The question of how to change the Iranian regime, or, failing that, the regime's murderous behavior, was never seriously addressed.

Reagan is now universally viewed as a tough guy, the man who beat the Soviet empire, the man who ordered the bombing of Libya in response to a terrorist attack in West Germany, and the man who approved the dramatic midair capture of the Palestinian terrorists who murdered an American invalid on an Italian cruise ship in the Mediterranean. But there was little sign of this toughness with regard to Iran. Indeed, in response to the massive killing of American diplomats and military personnel in Lebanon in 1983, Reagan merely approved a token bombing run—which everyone knew would do no real damage to the terrorists—and then simply pulled out. Years later, former FBI director Louis Freeh bitterly remarked that Iran sent "its surrogates, the Lebanese Hezbollah, to murder 241 Marines in their Beirut barracks. The U.S. response to that 1983 outrage was to pull our military forces out of the region. Such timidity was not lost upon Tehran."[5]

Ironically, the one American action that most dramatically changed Iranian behavior was an accident. On July 3, 1988, the USS *Vincennes*, erroneously believing it was under attack, shot down an Iranian passenger jet. This had a devastating effect on the mullahs (it was impossible for them to believe that it was really an accident; they saw it as proof the United States had thrown its military might behind Iraq in the war). This impression was reinforced in October. Knowing that an American convoy would pass nearby within a few days, the Iranians put some mines in the Persian Gulf. One of these exploded against an American frigate, wounding ten navy men. The U.S. navy responded by attacking three Iranian oil platforms that had been used as staging points by the Revolutionary Guards, and the Iranians foolishly escalated the conflict, sending air and sea power into the area. The results were predictable:

> The Iranian missile boat *Joshan* started the battle by firing a U.S.-made Harpoon . . . missile at an American cruiser (it missed) and was immediately sunk in a hail of

---

[5] Louis J. Freeh, "Khobar Towers," *The Wall Street Journal*, June 23, 2006.

missiles and gunfire. Iranian small boats and a pair of F-4s also tried to strike . . . and several of the boats were sunk or damaged, as was one of the F-4s. Later, the Iranian frigate *Sahand* fired on planes from the USS *Enterprise* . . . the *Enterprise* aircraft immediately put two Harpoon missiles and four laser-guided bombs into the *Sahand*, sinking her. Finally, in a remarkable act of stupidity, the Iranians also sent out the frigate *Sabalan* . . . and it too fired three missiles at a passing American A-6 Intruder [which] promptly put a 500-pound laser-guided bomb neatly down the *Sabalan's* smokestack.[6]

On the same day, Iranian ground forces were smashed by the Iraqis in a major battle. Soon thereafter Khomeini "drank the bitter poison" and made peace with Saddam Hussein.

CLINTON

Bill Clinton's presidency saw virtually all these themes repeated, from the belief that Iranian moderates and pragmatists were prepared to strike a grand diplomatic bargain, to a surprising willingness to assist in arming the

---

[6] Pollack, *Persian Puzzle*, 229–31.

mullahs, and even enabling them to expand their strategic reach beyond the boundaries of their own region. It is all the more surprising because the original impulse of Clinton's Middle East policy was firmly anti-Iranian. That policy was defined as "dual containment," aimed at both Iran and Iraq, albeit with two very different strategies. Iraq was subjected to harsh sanctions and an intrusive inspection regime; Iran was to be the object of bilateral and multilateral efforts to convince the mullahs to behave in more civilized ways. Change their behavior, not their regime, as the slogan went.

That this sort of moral suasion was destined to fail should have been obvious from the outset. Nor were we likely to convince our European friends to join in a serious sanctions program; during the years of Bush the Father the United States had become the largest single market for Iranian crude, and by Clinton's third year we were Iran's number three trading partner. Europeans were hardly likely to take seriously American requests that they cut back on business with the mullahs. Worse still, we covertly facilitated Iranian action in the Balkans.

The UN Security Council had imposed an arms embargo on both sides in the Serbia-Bosnia war, hoping thereby to stop the fighting. It didn't work and distinctly favored the Serbs, who had an easy time getting all the weapons they wanted. There were congressional efforts to end our adherence to the arms embargo, on the grounds that we should be willing to permit the Muslim government in Sarajevo to defend itself against the widely discussed Serbian campaign of ethnic cleansing.

The president viscerally sympathized with the congressional position, but feared the consequences of a unilateral American departure from the UN position. Clinton accordingly resorted to the same sort of secret diplomacy that had defined the Iran-Contra Affair. Croatia (actually half of Croatia, in the person of President Tudjman; the government was deeply divided over whether it should arm the Bosnians) had offered to serve as a middleman for Iranian weapons to the Bosnians and asked the United States to express its opinion. In April 1994, Clinton told our man in Croatia, Ambassador Peter Galbraith, to pointedly tell the Croatians that he had "no instructions" about the weapons shipments. Everybody thought that the Croatians would correctly interpret this as a clear "go" from Washington, but it didn't go as smoothly as we hoped.

Galbraith had quietly met with a Croatian official widely believed to have been an Iranian agent and had pushed hard for the Iranian "solution." Now he had his moment. He gave Tudjman the "no instructions" message, but the Croatian leader did not react. He seemed not to understand the import of the American's words, so

Galbraith patiently spelled it out: "Pay attention to what I did not say." That finally sank home, and the shipments began. The booty was evenly split between the Croats and the Bosnians, in keeping with a new federation that had been engineered by the United States.

Just as George Shultz, Bill Casey, and Caspar Weinberger were kept in the dark about the Iran initiative until quite late in the day, so Warren Christopher, Jim Woolsey, and William Perry were only let in on the secret after the fact. The CIA was particularly upset because this looked like a replay of the White House's secret diplomacy with Iran during the Reagan years. However, relations between the CIA and the White House were notoriously poor (Woolsey achieved only two one-on-one meetings with the president in his two years of service at Langley), and since there was no Agency involvement in the affair, nobody protested, even though the station chief in Croatia went ballistic, fearing we were replaying Iran-Contra.

The usual congressional investigations were launched, but in the end, in yet another echo of the Reagan years, even the most hostile members of the oversight committees were unable to demonstrate that any criminal action had been taken. They were certainly right; the problem was policy, not legality, and the consequences of the secret Bosnian policy were quite dire. Once the "go" was given, the Iranians swarmed into Bosnia. The weapons shipments were organized by the Revolutionary Guards, and its officers slid smoothly into the ranks of the Bosnian military. Iranian intelligence agents poured into Sarajevo and spread out, buying influence, recruiting agents, and establishing the usual network of charitable and educational institutions that spread the Khomeinist doctrine to the next generation of Muslims. As the House select subcommittee investigating the matter put it in unusually dramatic language:

> The Iranian intelligence service [VEVAK] ran wild through the area developing intelligence networks, setting up terrorist support systems, recruiting terrorist "sleeper" agents and agents of influence, and insinuating itself with the Bosnian political leadership to a remarkable degree. The Iranians effectively annexed large portions of the Bosnian security apparatus [known as the Agency for Information and Documentation (AID)] to act as their intelligence and terrorist surrogates. This extended to the point of jointly planning terrorist activities. The Iranian embassy became the largest in Bosnia and its officers were given unparalleled privileges and access at every level of the Bosnian government.[7]

---

[7] House Select Subcommittee to Investigate the United States Role in Iranian Arms Transfers to Croatia and Bosnia, *Final Report*, 201.

It was indeed Dr. Frankenstein's monster. Ungrateful as ever, the Iranians went to work building a network to fulfill their cry of "Death to America." Iranian agents started surveilling the American embassy in Zagreb, and American officials, especially those working for the CIA, received Iranian death threats and had to leave the country. And the hell of it was that there had been no compelling reason to turn to Iran for weapons; other, friendlier countries, such as Saudi Arabia, were quite willing to help their fellow Muslims.[8]

The monster Iranian operation in Bosnia could never have happened without America opening the door, and it opened the door to hell. Omar Abd al-Rahman, the "blind sheikh" who commanded the bombing attack on the Twin Towers in 1993, worked closely with a phony Bosnian humanitarian organization (Third World Relief Agency) that served as a cover for terrorist financing. The same agency was caught trying to smuggle weapons into Bosnia from Sudan in 1992. The Bosnian government, or at least important parts of it, helped several of the Al Qaeda terrorists involved in the 9/11 conspiracy, starting with Osama bin Laden himself, who, along with several of his henchmen, was given a Bosnian passport at

---

[8] Maud S. Beelman, "Fingerprints," *The New Republic*, October 28, 1996.

the embassy in Vienna in 1993. Mohammed Atta trained in Bosnia, which was the starting point for his suicide mission; from there he went to Hamburg, and thence to the United States. Two other 9/11 terrorists—Ramzi Binalshibh and Said Bahaji—were recruited into Al Qaeda by Mohammed Haydar Zammar, who ran a terrorist base in Bosnia. German investigators suspected that Zammar had also recruited Atta to the cause.[9]

Iran's role in running many of the jihadist training camps in Bosnia is beyond doubt. Investigators found a training manual at one of the camps written in Farsi and produced by the Islamic Republic. As a Serbian expert has written, "The Iranian regime has long been known as a financier and sponsor of terrorists exported all over the world, especially in the Balkans. It is well-known that Iran sent a Revolutionary Guards unit to Bosnia-Herzegovina, and their secret service . . . has established and helped train the Bosnian Muslim secret service (AID)."[10]

During the same period, the Clinton administration was trying to restrict Russian and Chinese arms shipments to Iran, a worthy effort that was typically on the agenda of the ongoing high-level talks between Vice Pres-

---

[9] Darko Trifunovic, "Terrorism and the Western Balkans: Al Qaeda's Global Network and Its Influence on Western Balkan Nations" (unpublished MS).
[10] Ibid.

ident Al Gore and Russian Prime Minister Victor Chernomyrdin. To this end, Gore and Chernomyrdin agreed in June 1995 that, while existing contracts between Russia and Iran could be honored, all Russian transfers to the Islamic Republic had to be terminated by the end of 1999. A secret aide-mémoire was signed to that effect on June 30.

There were at least two problems with the agreement, one of which no doubt caused the vice president some personal agony: it was manifestly in direct conflict with a law of which he was cosponsor, the Iran-Iraq Non-Proliferation Act of 1992, commonly known as the Gore-McCain Act. That law required the imposition of sanctions for "destabilizing" arms sales to either of the named countries, and the Russian Kilo-class submarine promised to Tehran was nothing if not that. Moreover, in 1996 Congress had enacted an amendment to the 1962 Foreign Assistance Act, requiring the imposition of sanctions on any country sending weapons to state sponsors of terrorism; Iran certainly met that requirement as well.

Finally, in December 1995, Gore and Chernomyrdin also agreed to keep secret the details of Russia's assistance to the Iranian nuclear program, an issue that would increasingly disturb the international community. In what Bill Gertz of the *Washington Times* later described as a "classified 'Dear Al' letter," Chernomyrdin said there was nothing new in the Russian/Iranian program, which he insisted was limited to training Iranian technicians in Moscow, and providing fuel for the Bushehr reactor for a ten-year period starting in 2001. It was therefore odd that the Russian letter stipulated that the information was not to be passed to third parties, and Chernomyrdin specified Congress as one such "third party."[11]

Chernomyrdin's concern for secrecy was explained by the classified American analysis that accompanied the government's copy of the letter; it flatly stated that if Russian assistance was not terminated, it would "only lead to Iran's acquisition of a nuclear weapons capability." Such a development, the analyst continued, "would be destabilizing not only for the already volatile Middle East, but would pose a threat to Russian and Western security interests."

Worse still, the Russians simply pocketed the agreement and went right on supporting the mullahs. The weapons shipments showed no sign of ending in late 1999, and it was increasingly obvious that Russian assistance to the Iranians on nuclear matters went well beyond the training of a few technicians and a promise of future uranium deliveries. Secretary of State Madeleine Albright was obliged to write an angry letter to her counterpart, Foreign Minister Igor Ivanov, in mid-January 2000, reminding him that the

---

[11] Bill Gertz, "Letter Shows Gore Made Deal," *The Washington Times*, October 17, 2000.

Clinton administration had gone out on a limb for the Russians: if we hadn't worked out that 1995 aide-mémoire, she pointedly remarked, "Russia's conventional arms sales to Iran would have been subject to sanctions based on various provisions of our law." She demanded a full accounting of "what has been delivered, what remains to be shipped, and anticipated timing" and requested that Moscow henceforth end their military relationship with the mullahs. If this did not happen, Russia's behavior would "unnecessarily complicate our relationship."

No doubt Igor Ivanov sent a reassuring letter to Ms. Albright, but as usual nothing much changed, to judge by events later that year. In October 2000, one Sergei Ivanov, the head of the Russian Security Council, proclaimed his country's strong conviction that there had to be "strong relations with Iran on many fronts."[12] This against a background of American accusations that the Russians were helping Iran with ballistic "and nuclear" missiles.

The U.S. government had once again enabled the Islamic Republic to build up its inventory of modern weaponry and expand its strategic reach. Like its predecessors, the Clinton administration was lured into doing things to which it was publicly and politically opposed

---

[12] "Russian Security Chief Hails Growing Ties with Iran," Agence France Presse, October 18, 2000.

(Clinton himself had often denounced President George H. W. Bush for being "soft" on Iran and promised a much tougher policy). And like its predecessors, the Clinton administration labored mightily to convince itself that it had done nothing wrong. When the stories about Iranian arms deliveries to Bosnia and Russian armaments to Tehran broke in the American press in 2000, the vice president's office angrily insisted that everything had been legal. But even if that was so, it was a bad mistake. Clinton's instincts about Iran were right, but his policies did nothing to make things better. Not even another bloody Iranian attack on American soldiers catalyzed a serious American policy. Quite the contrary, in fact.

KHOBAR TOWERS

On June 25, 1996, terrorists from the Saudi branch of Hezbollah, under direct control from Tehran, killed nineteeen American airmen in a dormitory in Dhahran, Saudi Arabia. Hundreds of other Americans were wounded, and a still unknown number of Saudi civilians, unluckily located in a local park, were killed or maimed.

There were good reasons to believe the Iranians were behind the slaughter; six of the terrorists were captured and confessed they had received training from the RG in the usual camps in the Bekáa Valley of Lebanon, had been paid a quarter of a million dollars by an RG general, and had been provided with passports by the Iranian embassy in Damascus. But the FBI, whose director, Louis Freeh, was put in charge of the investigation, only had this secondhand, from Saudi investigators. Over the next several months, the Saudis provided more such information. The Saudi ambassador to the United States, Bandar, told Freeh, "We have the goods," pointing "ineluctably toward Iran." The culprits were the usual suspects: Hezbollah, under direction from the Iranian Revolutionary Guards and the Iranian Ministry of Intelligence. And then there was a confession from outgoing Iranian president Hashemi Rafsanjani to Crown Prince Abdullah (at the time, effectively the Saudi king): "The Khobar attack had been planned and carried out with the knowledge of the Iranian supreme ruler, Ayatollah Khamenei."

The information was extremely explosive, but it was not nearly good enough, either for the FBI (which needed firsthand testimony or convincing physical evidence to indict and prosecute the terrorists and their puppeteers) or for the intelligence community, which had long since adopted the view that the U.S. government needed the same quality of evidence in order to take action. Government lawyers typically warn against taking any action, and rare is the leader who trusts his own judgment more than his lawyers. So Clinton, National Security Adviser Sandy Berger, and Director of Central Intelligence George Tenet insisted that we could not respond against Iran until and unless we had evidence that would lead a jury to convict the Islamic Republic. That evidence could only come from the Saudis, and they would not volunteer it; Freeh was repeatedly told by Saudis one step removed from the king that the evidence could be provided—by making the jailed terrorists available for questioning by the FBI—but only if President Clinton made a personal request for it.

Two fairly detailed, albeit quite different, accounts explain what happened next, and why. One comes from Kenneth Pollack, who was on the National Security Council staff, with special responsibility for Iranian matters. The other comes from Freeh himself. Pollack says the Saudis just didn't want to give us the information, at least for several years, even though—or perhaps because—Clinton was prepared to take military action against Iran if the case was strong enough. Freeh insists that the president did not raise the matter in his many conversations with the Saudis and is convinced that the Clinton White House did not really want to see the evidence, because it would have forced the United States to act . . . and when push came to shove, Clinton's wasn't prepared to do that.

"It soon became clear," Freeh insists, "that Mr. Clinton and his national security adviser, Sandy Berger, had no interest in confronting the fact that Iran had blown up the Towers." Freeh kept on writing talking points for Berger and Clinton to raise with the Saudi royal family, but to no avail. Freeh was told by the Saudis that neither Berger nor the president asked for anything, over a period of two and a half years. Indeed, Freeh acidly writes that Berger never even asked Freeh—over five years—about the progress of the investigation.

Pollack tells a very different story. In his view, the Saudis were conflicted and divided and could not decide if they really wanted us to take action against Iran. Indeed, they were so timorous that, just two months after the Khobar bombing, they turned down an American request to use Saudi air bases to stage an air assault against Saddam's Iraq following an Iraqi attack on the Kurdish city of Irbil, then under American protection. As Pollack says, "if the Saudis didn't even have the stomach for a military reprisal against Saddam, how could anyone expect them to give us information that would oblige us to strike the Islamic Republic?"[13] Pollack describes a time when Berger was asked by one of the top Saudis if the United States would bomb Iran if the information was

---

[13] Pollack, *Persian Puzzle*, 280ff.

provided to Washington. Berger smartly said he couldn't promise anything regarding information he hadn't seen, a snappy answer that was too clever by half; everyone knew what the terrorists had said and would presumably repeat if asked by the Americans.

The two versions can perhaps be reconciled. By the time Freeh was writing those talking points, the Saudis had already turned thumbs-down on the Iraqi operation, and Clinton and Berger could very well have drawn Pollack's conclusion: it was pointless to ask these people because they obviously weren't going to do it. The one thing certain was that the FBI didn't get access to the terrorists until the spring of 1999, and Freeh was in a position to know how that happened, since he masterminded it himself.

Freeh asked former president Bush, who had long-standing friendships with the most important members of the royal family, if he could raise the question with Crown Prince Abdullah. Armed with the usual talking points, Bush asked Abdullah to permit the FBI access to the terrorists. Shortly thereafter, Freeh was informed by the Saudi ambassador to Washington, Prince Bandar, that the request was granted. Within weeks, FBI agents interviewed the prisoners and got the evidence they had been begging for. At which point Freeh and Attorney General Janet Reno went to the White House with the news. Berger was decidedly not happy with the news. "Who knows about this?" he demanded. Then he organized some meetings. Then silence. "After those meetings, neither the president, nor anyone else in the administration, was heard from again about Khobar."

Things had changed, and both Pollack and Freeh agree on the reason: the election of Mohammad Khatami as president of the Islamic Republic in May 1997. No expert expected this to happen, since Khatami was relatively unknown and was described as a "reformer," the latest version of the phantasmagoric Iranian "moderates" so dear to the hearts of the Reagan optimists who'd traveled to Tehran ten years before. It should have been obvious that Khatami could not possibly have been a true reformer, for such a person would never have been permitted to acquire real power in the mullahcracy. The senior mullahs—known hard-liners—purged the proposed candidates list of all suspect persons. More than two hundred such candidates were eliminated before the guardians of Islam permitted Khatami's name to appear on the ballot, showing that he was one of them, not an opposition figure.

To be sure, the huge vote for Khatami was a vote against the hard-liners; no question about it. But Khatami was simply the empty political vessel into which the oppressed Iranian people poured their rage at the regime.

Some Iranians, constitutionally given to seeing a hidden hand at work where error and accident are the more likely explanations, believe that Khatami was a cunning deception engineered by the mullahs to trick both the Iranian people and the United States. By proclaiming himself a true reformer, he would flush out dissenters from all walks of life, enabling the regime to crush them. It's unlikely, but the two objectives were nonetheless accomplished. The year after Khatami's election, with protesters gaining mass with every passing month, there was a terrible purge of students, intellectuals, and political critics of the regime.

These dreadful actions were largely overlooked in Washington. The Clinton administration, which had contemplated a military strike against Iran in response to Khobar and the massacre of the Kurds in Irbil, turned on a dime. Within relatively short order, the Americans bought into the notion that Khatami wanted and was politically powerful enough to achieve a liberalization of the Islamic Republic, both domestically and internationally. To accomplish this miracle, the reformers around Khatami needed help from Washington. This meant that serious action against Iran was off the table, since nasty actions would only damage Khatami's presumed actions to moderate the behavior of the regime and move toward reconciliation with America. Instead of studying military scenarios, the Clinton people looked for ways to charm the mullahs.

Ever willing to contemplate a deal, and ever seeking yet another bonanza from Washington without having to sacrifice any vital interest of their own, the Iranians were only too happy to promise they'd move in that direction, if only we would be sufficiently generous. To show our goodwill, we opened a channel of communications to the highest levels of the regime—primarily to Khatami and former president Rafsanjani—and made several significant concessions to the Iranians. We liberalized our visa policies and expanded cultural exchanges, for example, permitting our wrestlers to travel to Iran to participate in the world championships. This had the consequence of creating even more problems with the FBI.

Secretary of State Madeleine Albright and Mr. Clinton ordered the FBI to stop photographing and fingerprinting Iranian wrestlers and cultural delegations entering the U.S. because the Iranians were complaining about the identification procedure. Of course they were complaining. It made it more difficult for their MOIS agents and terrorist coordinators to infiltrate into America. I was overruled by an "angry" president and Mr. Berger, who said the FBI was interfering with their rapprochement with Iran.[14]

---

[14] Freeh, "Khobar Towers."

We placed the Iranians' bogeyman, the Mujahedin e-Khalq (MEK) organization (which carried out paramilitary operations from Iraq into Iran), on our official list of terrorist organizations. We shamefully removed the Islamic Republic from the State Department's list of state sponsors of terrorism, and from the list of narco-trafficking governments. We permitted American companies to sell food and medicine to Iranian purchasers. Secretary of State Madeleine Albright went to international talks on the future of Afghanistan, hoping she would be able to talk directly to Iranian foreign minister Kharrazi, and in April 1999 President Clinton himself delivered an unscripted soliloquy at a White House dinner in which he regretted past American actions with regard to Iran. "I think sometimes it's quite important to tell people, look, you have a right to be angry at something my country or my culture or others that are generally allied with us today did to you fifty or sixty or one hundred or one hundred and fifty years ago. But that is different from saying that I am outside the faith, and you are God's chosen."[15]

It wasn't a formal apology—that came eleven months later—but, against the background of concessions it was a dramatic gesture. All for naught. Indeed, as Pollack

---

[15] Pollack, *Persian Puzzle*, 323.

notes, Iraqi oil was being smuggled through Iranian waters in open defiance of the embargo on Iraq. But the Clinton folks went even further. On March 17, 2000, Secretary Albright openly apologized for our alleged sins against the Islamic Republic:

> The United States played a significant role in orchestrating the overthrow of Iran's popular prime minister, Mohammed Mossadegh . . . the coup was clearly a setback for Iran's political development . . . the United States gave sustained backing to the shah's regime . . . [which] brutally repressed political dissent . . . the United States must bear its fair share of responsibility for the problems that have arisen in U.S.-Iranian relations . . . aspects of U.S. policy towards Iraq during its conflict with Iran appear now to have been regrettably shortsighted.

One is far more likely to hear complaints about Mossadegh's overthrow from Iranian leftists than from followers of Khomeini, but official Iranians invariably complain about it, probably because it restored their enemy, the hated shah, to the throne. In any event, it no doubt seemed obligatory to the secretary of state to apologize for all past sins, not merely those committed against the mullahs, and she may well have felt guilty for America's role in the ouster of Mossadegh.

For extras, Albright pled guilty to a crime we had certainly not committed. She apologized for favoring Iraq in the war. It's a pretty amazing claim, given the quantity of arms and money and intelligence we showered on Iran in an effort to ransom our hostages. For the Iranians, the shootdown of the Iran Air passenger plane by the USS *Vincennes* was the decisive fact. No Iranian could possibly accept that it was an accident, even though it was.

All those gestures and concessions and giveaways yielded the usual result: insults from Tehran. Supreme Leader Ali Khamenei delivered one of his patented diatribes: "What do you think the Iranian nation, faced with this situation and these admissions, feels? . . . What good will this admission [of supporting Saddam in the war with Iran]—that you acted in that way then—do us now? . . . An admission years after the crime was committed, while they might be committing similar crimes now, will not do the Iranian nation any good."

Pollack thinks that if Khatami-the-reformer had had more power, or more courage, the grand bargain might have been negotiated. But that ignores the nature of the Islamic Republic. Khatami was effectively powerless; real power resided with the Supreme Leader (there is a reason for that title), and Khamenei didn't want any part of a deal with the Great Satan. The American strategy, then as now, was based on an illusion: that the Islamic Republic could renounce terrorism, perhaps treat its own people better, and ultimately become a normal country.

The simple unpleasant truth is that it is hard to find a historical case in which a revolutionary regime has voluntarily and successfully moderated its behavior. Regime change is necessary for that to happen, and Bill Clinton, like all American presidents since Jimmy Carter, never seriously contemplated that.

GEORGE W. BUSH

The Bush administration's policy toward Iran was driven by the events of 9/11. Iran was famously included in the tripartite "Axis of Evil" (Iran, Iraq, and North Korea) against which our war on terrorism would be waged, and it could hardly be otherwise. Year after year, the State Department had put Iran at the top of its list of state sponsors of terrorism. Once the president declared that we would not distinguish between terrorists and the states that supported them, Iran was automatically a prime target. Moreover, President Bush embraced pro-democracy regime change as the core of his antiterrorist strategy. Both the terrorists and their state sponsors were tyrannical, hence successful democratic revolution would greatly reduce the threat.

It is widely believed that Bush's foreign policy was decisively defined by people who had long wanted to strike
down Saddam Hussein—and perhaps use military power
against Iran as well. According to this view, which has
achieved canonical status on both ends of the political
spectrum, the "neoconservatives" had sway over the president from the moment the first plane flew into the World
Trade Center in lower Manhattan. This may have been
true about Iraq policy, but never about Iran. Even though
the president's many words (supporting the "legitimate desire of the Iranian people to be free") seemed to presage a
vigorous campaign against the mullahs, no such policy
was ever carried out. Whatever impulse he may have had
along such lines, there was a formidable coalition against
it, including Secretary of State Colin Powell, Deputy Secretary Richard Armitage, National Security Adviser Condoleezza Rice, and the director of the policy planning
staff at State, Richard Haass, who believed, as so many
before him, that the moment had come to strike a grand
bargain with the mullahs. If that were not enough, Director of Central Intelligence George Tenet—a holdover
from the Clinton administration—acted as if he did not
want to know the full extent of hostile Iranian actions
against us and our Lebanese and Israeli allies, thereby de-
priving the White House of information that might have
helped crystallize a coherent policy.

The first move was forced: Afghanistan. Al Qaeda was there, and Al Qaeda had to be destroyed, therefore we attacked less than two months after 9/11, shattered Al Qaeda, and set about establishing order. As we did so, the mullahs feigned friendship at the negotiating table. At a series of international and regional conferences, Iranian diplomats cooperated with their American counterparts on the structure of the new Afghanistan, and by all accounts they were exceedingly forthcoming. At the same time, in a classic deception, the Iranians organized terrorist squads to kill our soldiers inside Afghanistan. According to firsthand information given to Pentagon officials by knowledgeable Iranians, the Revolutionary Guards had trained and armed terrorists who were ordered to attack coalition troops. The information was quite precise, including the locations from which the terrorists would operate. It was passed on to U.S. Special Forces, who eliminated the threat.

I was present at the interviews that produced that information, which the Iranian sources promised was only the first of a considerable quantity of detailed intelligence about the mullahs' capabilities and intentions. There was every reason to expect the American government would want to continue the conversations; after all, those Iranians had saved American lives once, and it was reasonable to hope they might well save more in the future. But not only was there no interest in following up with the proven sources of reliable information—not so easy to come by, after all—there was outright hostility from both the CIA and the State Department. News of the meetings (which had taken place in Rome) was leaked to the press, insinuating something untoward had happened, and Powell and Tenet demanded an end to all such contacts. A few months later, when Tenet reviewed the matter and decided it would be prudent to resume the dialogue, Powell again railed against it. New leaks followed within days, and Secretary of Defense Donald Rumsfeld joined the party, ordering all Pentagon personnel to terminate contacts with Iranians. One Iranian-American in the Defense Department plaintively asked if this included parents and other close relatives living in the area.

Louis Freeh would have recognized this pattern of behavior; it was a replay of the reaction to Khobar Towers. Just as proof of Iranian complicity was unwelcome because it threatened the Clinton administration's desire to achieve rapprochement with Iran, so proof of Iranian-sponsored attacks against Americans in Afghanistan threatened the desires of many policymakers and diplomats to build on their happy experiences around international conference tables.

The Bush administration tread the same path as the

others, organizing meetings (sometimes using former American officials, sometimes staff members of the National Security Council, sometimes private citizens with no diplomatic pedigree) with Iranian intermediaries and midlevel officials, transmitting messages through the Swiss embassy in Tehran, constantly looking for possible areas of cooperation, hoping for the big breakthrough that predictably never arrived. Like the Clinton people, Bush's advisers were probably hypnotized by the spectacle of "reformist" President Khatami, even though he authorized some of the worst human rights violations, and even though he oversaw a worrisome acceleration of the nuclear program, as Israel's top analyst warned just a few weeks after Bush came into office.

> Iran and Iraq appear to be just a few years away from attaining atomic bomb capability, according to Dr. Dany Shoham, an expert on weapons of mass destruction in the Middle East arena. . . . In both cases, the regimes apparently still lack adequate quantities of fissile material—enriched military-grade uranium or plutonium—necessary for producing atomic bombs. Iran and Iraq are making intensive efforts to produce this material by domestic application of existing technologies, while seeking ways of acquiring it from other countries.

Shoham said that if either was able to achieve this, they could conceivably have nuclear bombs or atomic warheads within a year.[16]

Shoham pointed out that Iran had plenty of international support, had already developed a medium-range missile, and was therefore better placed than Iraq to combine a nuclear warhead with an accurate missile. And he noted that Iran was working hard on chemical and biological weapons as well.

We went to war against Iraq at least in part because we believed Saddam was developing, or actually possessed, weapons of mass destruction. Publicly available information on Iran showed the same was true of the Islamic Republic. In the end, the Bush administration's response to the Iranian nuclear threat was limited to diplomacy: we joined with Great Britain, France, and Germany in years of fruitless negotiations aimed at convincing the Iranians to give up their nuclear program, even though they constantly told us they would not do it. Moreover, the logic of the war against terrorism led to the conclusion that Iran should be confronted. We knew that Iran had organized

---

[16] David Rudge, *Jerusalem Post*, February 26, 2001, http://www.jpost.com/Editions/2001/02/26/News/News.22017.html.

the killing of Americans in Saudi Arabia in 1996, in East Africa in 1998, and in Afghanistan in 2001. But we continued to look for a diplomatic "solution" that had proven unattainable for more than twenty years.

We are too close to the events to have proper perspective, but future scholars will almost surely marvel at the fact that, as of the spring of 2007—which is to say, nearly six and a half years after taking office, and five and a half years after 9/11—the Bush administration still had no formal Iran policy and, like its predecessors, had not effectively responded to the ongoing Iranian war against us. It was perhaps not surprising that Bush, Powell, Rice, et al. failed to reverse the long-standing American practice of giving the Iranians the diplomatic equivalent of a free pass for their many hostile actions. The surprise came from the considerable divergence between the declarations of the president and his top aides, and the administration's lack of action.

The old sarcastic lyric about philosophers, "for, he argued, razor-witted, that can't be which is not admitted," is particularly appropriate for the Bush administration's groping for a successful Iran policy. In part, the failure was due to the process installed by National Security Adviser Rice. Each president has his own methods for establishing his administration's policy. There are often disputes among his cabinet secretaries, and only the president can resolve them. Some presidents—Reagan, for example—asked the National Security Council to define the disagreements as precisely as possible, then bring them to the chief executive. Bush did not want that; he wanted a harmonious policy process, and he asked that every effort be made to resolve disputes before he was asked to make a final decision. Rice, therefore, invariably instructed her subordinates to look for some middle ground, some compromise to which all could agree. This prolonged the process, sometimes over long periods, as the issues were debated by the cabinet members' deputies, memos were written and rewritten, and no guidance came down from the Oval Office.

Even during the happiest times, American governments, as the American people, are fractious; if decisions are not made and enforced, the various players pursue their own favorite policies as hard as they can, hoping that they can accomplish something worthwhile before somebody tells them to stop. In the case of Iran policy, this meant that the State Department, along with members of the National Security Council staff, with added support from key officials in the intelligence community, pursued détente with Iran.

Most people who follow American foreign policy are

astonished to learn that Clinton's quest for rapprochement with Iran continued under Bush, but the evidence is easily available in the popular press. In an interview with the *Los Angeles Times* in mid-February 2003—subsequently confirmed by the State Department—Deputy Secretary of State Richard Armitage proved the point: "I would note that there's one dramatic difference between Iran and the other two members of the axis of evil . . . they're a democracy, so I think you approach a democracy differently."

This sort of statement, so clearly at odds with the nature of the Islamic Republic, is always intended as a "signal." Armitage was telling the Iranians—on the eve of the invasion of Iraq—that they were not slated for an American attack. And despite repeated criticism of Iran over the subsequent four years, there was no hint that the United States would do anything other than talk. Even in his second term, when many expected Bush would take the gloves off and promote regime change, he continued to press for diplomatic solutions, plus a few limited sanctions when the mullahs refused to end their nuclear enrichment program. In late 2006, for example, the president told a news conference, "We've got a lot of issues with Iran. . . . The first is whether or not they will help this young democracy [Iraq] succeed." The "second issue" was whether Iran would help the Lebanese government, and the "big issue" was "whether or not Iran will end up with a nuclear weapon."[17]

This was on a par with Armitage's remark. No one could possibly believe that the mullahs might help Iraq succeed: their definition of "success" is the humiliation of America and the domination of Iraq. Nor could any serious person believe that Iran might help the Lebanese government: Iranian policy called for the destruction of the elected government, the slaughter or domination of the Maronite Christians, and the creation of an Islamic Republic under the thumb of Hezbollah. Finally, the claim that the nuclear question was the "big issue" was itself dubious. American lives were being taken in Iraq and Afghanistan by Iranian weapons, killers, and managers. Most Americans would probably consider that a bigger issue than a secret program the CIA kept saying would not reach fulfillment for a decade or so.

Bush's words and tone about the "issues" between America and the Islamic Republic were of a piece with those of Secretary of State Rice. She gave a long interview to Bret Stephens of *The Wall Street Journal* at about

---

[17] Michael Ledeen, "Iran & W," *National Review Online*, October 30, 2006.

the same time as the president's press conference. The interview was unusually candid and distinctly pessimistic. She was reluctant to describe the life-and-death conflict in the Middle East as a "war," preferring to call it a "battle, if you will, or a struggle." She did not expect the United States to win it during the Bush presidency, and she saw her mission for the remaining two years of Bush's term as "put[ting] some fundamentals in place."[18]

To be sure, she insisted that the terrorists had to be defeated, but she then oddly omitted American national security from her description of why it was so important to win in Iraq: "We just have to fight tooth and nail for the victory of the Iraqis who do not want Iranian influence in their daily lives." This was doubly notable, first because she didn't say that our children had to fight for us, and our future, but rather for the Iraqis. Did she not know that the Iranians were trying to massacre the Americans in Iraq and Afghanistan? And it was also notable because she defined the war in Iraq as a battle against "Iranian influence in [Iraqis'] daily lives."

No major publication or analyst thought it newsworthy that the secretary of state had defined the battle (or struggle) in Iraq in terms of Iranian aggression against

---

[18] Bret Stephens, "Secretary of Turbulence," *Wall Street Journal*, September 30, 2006.

Iraq. Indeed, she went even further, expressing real urgency about the Iranian assault: "We've got a chance to resist the Iranian push into the region, but we better get about it. I mean, it's not the sort of thing that you can just let continue in its current form."

No top official in any Western government had previously suggested that Iran was the driving force behind the terror war in Iraq, so her statement warranted front-page coverage. Moreover, it coincided with the recent declaration by Major General Richard Zahner (Deputy Chief of Staff for Intelligence with Multinational Force Iraq) that "Iran is definitely a destabilizing force. . . . Iran is responsible for training, funding, and equipping some of these Shia extremist groups."

The other important point in the interview was Rice's recognition that Iraq was just one part of "the Iranian push into the region," suggesting that the administration had a clear picture of the regional nature of the war, and of Iran's role throughout the area. But then, having identified the central issue, she backed away from the logical response: firm action against the mullahs. As Bret Stephens sadly observed, the only reaction she proposed was to take the whole ugly mess to the United Nations and other multinational diplomatic forums. "The international system will agree on a level of pressure. I think it will evolve over time." She insisted that the diplomatic option looked better than ever, said the Europeans have been "very strong on this," and expressed hope that sanctions would have an effect on Iranian officials who "do not want to endure the kind of isolation that they're headed toward." Stephens, surprised that Rice apparently thought there were legitimate interlocutors in power in Tehran, pressed her, and she responded, "I do not believe we're going to find Iranian moderates. . . . The question is, are we going to find Iranian reasonables?"

In short, neither she nor the president had any serious intention of challenging the Tehran regime. She did not mention that the Islamic Republic has been waging war against us for twenty-eight years, during which time we have offered them every imaginable deal (she herself trotted out a long list of "incentives" if they agreed to suspend their nuclear enrichment program). They have rejected every one. But she was still hunting for "reasonables," the great white whale of American diplomacy ever since the Islamic Revolution of 1979.

It is impossible not to be struck by the cognitive dissonance between this interview and the many speeches by the president in which he all but called for regime change in Iran. There are several ways to interpret this dissonance. The first is that the administration really did have a plan, but did not believe public opinion was yet ready to support it and was trying to build at least the basis for a consensus on the tougher action the president intended to take. Thus, Rice's description of Iranian action in Iraq and elsewhere in the region. Thus, General Zahner's categorical fingering of the mullahs. Thus, the president's many speeches.

Alternatively, the president and his secretary of state may have believed that time was on our side, that the world was moving toward serious action against Iran, and that if we were only patient enough and played our diplomatic cards well, we would be part of meaningful multinational sanctions against Tehran that would finally solve the problem.

Finally, it may be that Bush and Rice did not fully appreciate what the Iranians were up to, that they had not recognized that the Islamic Republic had committed several acts of war against us. As Bob Woodward tells us in his latest book, *State of Denial*,[19] some American officials acted on at least some occasions to prevent the president from hearing about these acts of war:

Pages 414–415: "Some evidence indicated that the Iranian-backed terrorist group Hezbollah was training insurgents to build and use the shaped IEDs, at the urging of the Iranian Revolutionary Guards Corps. That

---

[19] Bob Woodward, *State of Denial* (New York: Simon & Schuster, 2006).

kind of action was arguably an act of war by Iran against the United States. If we start putting out everything we know about these things, Zelikow felt, the administration might well start a fire it couldn't put out."

Page 449: "The components and the training for [the IEDs] had more and more clearly been traced to Iran, one of the most troubling turns in the war."

Page 474: "The radical Revolutionary Guards Corps had asked Hezbollah, the terrorist organization, to conduct some of the training of Iraqis to use the EFPs, according to U.S. Intelligence. If all this were put out publicly, it might start a fire that no one could put out. . . . Second, if it were true, it meant that Iranians were killing American soldiers—an act of war."

Is it possible that President Bush is not aware of this history? Woodward's account shows that at least some policymakers (he cites Philip Zelikow, the counselor at State, but there are no doubt others as well) were reluctant to pass this information up the line to a president who could be expected to take action after he learned about it. Secretary of State Colin Powell was famously unwilling to give U.S. support to Iranian dissidents ("We don't want to get involved in an Iranian family squabble"), and there was Armitage's unfortunate description of the tyrannical Islamic Republic as a "democracy." They would not have wanted the president to know that there were frequent Iranian acts of war against American men and women on the battlefield.

What about the intelligence community? Are they not obliged to inform the president of Iranian acts of war? Indeed they are, but they, too, were concerned about the president's muscular foreign policy. In 2004, I was asked by a high-ranking intelligence officer to "take it easy on Iran" because, he thought, "things were going along nicely," and in a decade or so we could expect an Iranian democracy. But if we got engaged, "God only knows what will happen." I took that to mean that the Agency feared that, if the president knew all the things Iran was doing, he might call upon them to "do something." As mentioned earlier, in December 2001, Iranians meeting secretly with American officials in Rome informed us about Iranian plans to kill coalition soldiers in Afghanistan. In short order, orders were given to terminate all such contacts with Iranians. That, too, suggested that the CIA, in lockstep with the State Department, didn't want the president to know too much about Iran's war against us.

There is no doubt that high administration officials tried to prevent the president from getting facts proving that Iran was waging war against us. Part of this stemmed from the diplomats' long-standing obsession with solving the Iranian problem through negotiations, but there was another component, specific to the CIA. Everybody knows that the CIA's intelligence on Iraq was weak, but it was considerably better than its work on Iran, which was already unsatisfactory at the time of the Revolution and could only get worse thereafter. In the mideighties, for example, the Iran desk officer at the Agency was shockingly ignorant of the key figures in Tehran, having devoted most of his career to Latin American countries. As late as 2006, the head of the CIA team working on Iran was, as usual, an Arabist who did not speak or read Farsi. And the CIA's efforts to recruit agents in Iran were famously inept. On at least two occasions, Iranian counterintelligence rolled up "networks" of American agents. Things got so bad throughout the Middle East that, according to Reuel Gerecht (who spent nine years in the Operations Directorate with special emphasis on Iran), there came a time when the CIA would not send a lone officer to meet with a *possibly* dangerous foreigner. And as for infiltrating terrorist groups, another former CIA case officer put it nicely: "Operations that include diarrhea as a way of life don't happen."[20]

As a former Agency official drily put it, in many ways the CIA had become a cross between the Post Office and the Department of Agriculture. Yet George W. Bush, fol-

---

[20] Michael A. Ledeen, *The War Against the Terror Masters* (New York: St. Martin's Press, 2002), 124.

lowing in the footsteps of his father (who was briefly director of central intelligence), had great trust in the Agency's
information. This flew in the face of the Agency's manifest
failure to detect and dismantle the conspiracy that produced 9/11, but a president who believed the CIA had
failed would have fired Tenet and shaken up the leadership
of the entire intelligence community. Instead, no one was
fired, and indeed when Tenet retired, he was given the
highest award the president could bestow upon him. On all
accounts the two men got along well, which is one key to
the CIA's influence in the government (the other being
good relations with key congressional leaders).

So the CIA had a lot to say about American policy and
used its influence in many ways, some aggressive (such as
shutting down contacts with Iranians with information the
Agency didn't want on the president's desk), and others
quite subtle. One of their favorites is to set a high standard
for "proof" when the facts imply action should be taken. I
recall a meeting in the early eighties when a terrorist had
come from Damascus to Istanbul and gone straight from
the airport to attack a synagogue. When someone suggested we might do something to punish the Syrians, the
Agency representative said, "But we have no evidence the
Syrian government was involved in this." This same refrain was heard in late 2006 and early 2007, when the
American military had accumulated overwhelming evi-

dence that high-powered explosives, used to great effect against our troops in Iraq, had Iranian components and were being smuggled into Iraq across the Iranian border. Agency officials argued that this did not necessarily prove that the Iranian regime had ordered, or even approved, the operations (which were the single greatest cause of American fatalities). The line was echoed by Secretary of Defense Gates and by Chairman of the Joint Chiefs Pace, and the press was full of stories hinting that the Revolutionary Guards might be acting on their own, a sort of Iranian "rogue force" doing things the Supreme Leader might not like. No matter that the components had Iranian serial numbers that led to an official manufacturing facility, and no matter that the idea of RG "solo operations" was preposterous, since the Corps had specifically been created to be the creature of the Supreme Leader himself.

The policy implication of the "we don't know for sure that the leaders of the regime are responsible for this" argument is that the United States is therefore not entitled to take action against the regime. But that is nonsense; you don't need secret intelligence to know that the regime is at war with us, and therefore we must sooner or later respond. To know that, all you have to do is read any of the recent State Department "country reports" on Iran. Take the one published in 2005, for example: "Iran remained the most active state sponsor of terrorism in 2004. Its

Islamic Revolutionary Guards Corps and Ministry of Intelligence and Security were involved in the planning and support of terrorist acts and continued to exhort a variety of groups to use terrorism in pursuit of their goals."[21]

The State Department knows that Iranian claw marks are all over the terror war in Iraq and says so in its own peculiar, convoluted way: "Iran pursued a variety of policies in Iraq during 2004, some of which appeared to be inconsistent with Iran's stated objectives regarding stability in Iraq. . . . Senior [Iraqi] officials have publicly expressed concern over Iranian interference in Iraq, and there were reports that Iran provided funding, safe transit, and arms to insurgent elements."

In normal English, that would read, "Iran says it wants stability in Iraq, but it isn't so; the mullahcracy supports the terrorists." Had the State Department been interested in expanding its context ever so slightly, it could have added, "And its support for the terrorists is coordinated with the Syrians." A few months before the report was published, American forces in Iraq captured photographs and documents about a meeting in Syria between Iraqi terrorists and Syrian and Iranian intelligence officials. Similar information was found in Fallujah.

---

[21] Michael Ledeen, "The Hand of the Mullahs: What We Know, and What We Don't Do," *National Review Online*, May 4, 2005.

Like the rest of us, the president certainly knew enough to recognize the seriousness of the Iranian threat. He didn't pull in his horns because he was hoodwinked by the intelligence community; he made a policy decision based on the recommendations of his top advisers and his closest allies, and it was the same failed policy decision that had been made by every American president since Jimmy Carter.

Surely we can do better.

4　　HOW TO WIN

There are times in the long history of the human adventure when we have a real turning point, a major change—the end of an era, the beginning of a new era. I am becoming more and more convinced that we are in such an age at the present time—a change in history comparable with such events as the fall of Rome, the discovery of America, and the like.

—Bernard Lewis

Those who want to set up democracy want to drag our country into corruption and perdition. They are worse than the Jews. They must be hanged. They are not men. They have the blood of animals. Be they damned.

—Khomeini

According to Bernard Lewis, the Iranian war against the United States is a major component of a larger phenomenon: the third Muslim assault against the infidel West. Twice in the past, the Muslim armies made great progress, only to be rolled back. For the past two hundred years and more, the Muslim Middle East has been dominated by imperialist powers, but the Iranians and their allies in the global jihad believe the wheel has turned. In Osama bin Laden's view of recent history, two great imperialist forces dominated the Muslim world: the United States and the Soviet Union. Muslim jihadists defeated the tougher enemy in Afghanistan, which then collapsed. The Americans will be a lot easier. The jihadis, aided, abetted, trained, funded, and, in many cases, led by Iran, believe that a final victory is within their grasp. That is why Professor Lewis views this moment as a major turning point. If our enemies win, it will decisively change the world.

Some of the most thoughtful analysts of contemporary Iran believe that the Islamic Republic is currently in the throes of a second Islamic revolution, driven by Ahmadinejad and the Revolutionary Guards Corps from which he comes.[1] As the label suggests, Iranian leaders seek a revitalization of Khomeini's original vision—above all, the export of the revolution—and fully embrace "such events as 'destruction, pestilence, and wars,' which they see as the inevitable accompaniments of the Mahdi's

---

[1] Brigadier General (Ret.) Dr. Shimon Shapira and Daniel Diker, "Iran's Second Islamic Revolution: Strategic Implications for the West," in *Iran, Hizbullah, Hamas and the Global Jihad* (Jerusalem: Jerusalem Center for Public Affairs, 2007).

return. Amir Taheri terms this "a deliberate clash of civilizations with the West."[2]

The Iranian leaders believe they are favored by Allah, who is preparing to unleash the enormous power of the Mahdi, the twelfth Imam, who vanished from human sight many centuries ago, and whose return will signal the triumph of the faithful over all their enemies and bring mankind to the end of days, the Final Judgment, and the opening of paradise to all good Muslims. These beliefs are quite concrete, not only for uneducated Iranians, but for those who make decisions of state, including Supreme Leader Ali Khamenei, President Ahmadinejad, and many of their closest allies and advisers. In a cabinet meeting soon after Ahmadinejad's electoral victory in 2005, the new ministers printed, ratified, and signed an agreement with the twelfth Imam. In his opening remarks, Ahmadinejad's first deputy suggested that the cabinet ministers should sign such an agreement, just as they had signed a pact with the new president. The ministers agreed. But how to inform the Mahdi?

The solution was to ask the minister of culture and

---

[2] Amir Taheri, "A Clash of Civilizations," *Newsweek International*, September 5, 2005, http://www.msnbc.msn.com/id/9108626/site/newsweek/.

Islamic guidance to deliver the signed agreement to the Jamkaran well in the holy city of Qom, where the faithful believe the twelfth Imam is hiding, and where believers traditionally leave messages, prayers, and requests.

We are talking about some of the highest-ranking officials in the Islamic Republic, who believe that the Islamic Republic owes its legitimacy to a vanished religious figure at the bottom of a well in one of the most beautiful cities in the world. It's the twelfth Imam, not the people of Iran, who bestows power and authority. They are convinced that he will soon emerge, and they even think they know what he looks like. The official Web site of the Iranian broadcasting system laid it out on November 30, 2006:

> He will appear as a handsome young man, clad in neat clothes and exuding the fragrance of paradise. His face will glow with love and kindness for the human beings, and because of this reason a famous hadith from the Prophet of Islam (SAWA) has referred to him as Inn-al-Mahdi Tavous ahl al-Jannah, which means "indeed the Mahdi will be like a peacock among the people of paradise." He has a radiant forehead, black, piercing eyes, and a broad chest. He very much resembles his ancestor Prophet Muhammad (SAWA). Heavenly light and justice accompany him. He will overcome enemies and oppressors with the help of God, and as per the promise of the

Almighty, the Mahdi will eradicate all corruption and injustice from the face of the earth and establish the global government of peace, justice, and equity.

Like all believers in messianic movements, the Iranians and many (albeit not all) of their terrorist allies believe they are empowered by superhuman forces against which we are powerless. They think they are winning, and each and every success in the war confirms them in their belief that Allah has blessed their cause. Armed with this faith, they have indoctrinated millions of young fighters to rally to their cause and fight the infidels across the world. There is no way to negotiate a reasonable modus operandi with such people, since their war on us derives from ultimate issues, not geopolitical disagreements.

It is often said that the current war is a new kind of conflict because we are not fighting against traditional nation-states seeking to expand their domain at our expense, but against a transnational ideology that aims at the creation of a global caliphate. This theme has variously been described as a war of civilizations or a war of ideas, which we can only win if we somehow defeat or discredit our enemies' ideas. The president evidently shares this concern, for he put one of his most trusted advisers, Karen Hughes, in charge of the "war of ideas."

There is no doubt that the war on terror has an

important ideological component, but that hardly makes it unique. Indeed, in the last two global conflicts of the twentieth century—the Second World War and the Cold War—we fought two mass movements (fascism and communism) that were every bit as messianic as the clerical fascism we face today. In both cases, we were told that the "war of ideas" was paramount.

Many scholars and strategists at the time insisted that Nazism was first and foremost an ideology, not a state. Much like some of today's jihadists, Hitler was at pains to proclaim that he was fighting for an Aryan reich, not a German state. If you read some of the literature on Nazism, or, for that matter, the broader work on totalitarianism produced by the "greatest generation," you'll find a profound preoccupation with "winning the war of ideas" against fascism. We spent a lot of money and human energy, during and after the war, to denazify and defascistize the Old World.

When we smashed Hitler, Nazi ideology died along with him and fell into the same bunker.

The same debate over "Who or what are we fighting?" raged during the Cold War, when we debated whether we were fighting Communist ideology or Russian imperialism. Some saw the Cold War primarily in ideological terms and thought we would win if and only if we wooed the world's masses from the Communist dream. Others warned that this was an illusion, and that we'd better tend to "containment" lest the Red Army bring us and our allies to our knees.

When the Soviet empire fell, the appeal of communism fell with it.

Today's enemies are not totally different from those of the recent past; our wars against fascism and communism were waged against people whose wicked ideas came from Western culture, as do some of those chanted against us by Iran and the other terror masters. That virulent anti-Semitism at the core of the jihadists' worldview, the hatred of the Jews to which Khomeini gave voice and which is repeated almost daily by Khamenei and Ahmadinejad, is right out of the Führer's old playbook (which helps understand why jihad and the revival of anti-Semitism in Europe are running in tandem). To be sure, it is not simply an imposition of a noxious Western doctrine on an innocent Islamic culture; those anti-Semitic seeds took root in rich soil that had long nourished hatred of the Jews. There is certainly ample xenophobia in Islam, and Bat Ye'or's fine work on dhimmitude, and Robert Spencer's studies of Quranic anti-Semitism, abundantly document the Muslim drive to dominate the infidel, and above all the Jew. But the kind of rabid, racist anti-Semitism that we find in contemporary Middle Eastern gutters has a Western trademark. It started in France in the nineteenth century, got a pseudoscientific gloss from the Austrians and Germans a generation later, and spread like topsy.

We could not have won the Cold War or the Second World War by outdebating the communists and fascists. They saw that they'd lost the debate when they lost the war, and hundreds of millions of people around the world came to the same conclusion, for the same reason. In large measure, the claim that we must first win the ideological war in order to accomplish our mission against the terrorists is an intellectual and strategic trap. It diverts our attention and our energies from winning the war, and as the great strategic thinker Vince Lombardi reminds us, winning is the only thing.

The question is, how? The answer is, the same way we brought down the Soviet empire, by exporting the American democratic revolution, by adopting the methods that have successfully been used against dictators from Moscow and Belgrade to Beirut and the Philippines. The best strategy is to support the Iranian people against the mullahs they so hate.

A major military attack against Iran, of the sort we directed against Saddam's Iraq, would be a mistake; indeed, it would constitute a tragic admission of the failure of the

United States and our allies to conceive and conduct a serious Iran policy over nearly three decades. Political support for the tens of millions of Iranians who detest their tyrannical leaders is both morally obligatory and strategically sound. Perhaps 10 percent of Soviet citizens were willing to openly challenge the Kremlin; the Iranian regime's own public opinion polling shows that upward of 70 percent of Iranians want greater freedom and better relations with the United States. Even if all else were the same, how could anyone be pessimistic about the Iranians' ability to change their regime when they have at a minimum seven times the percentage of the population on the side of revolution as the pro-democracy Soviets had in the eighties? And things are not at all the same; unlike the gray public passivity that defined the Soviet people in the last decades of the empire, Iran bubbles with energy and confrontation between the rulers and their subjects; hardly a day goes by without strikes, demonstrations, and even the occasional armed attack against the mullahs and their instruments of repression. Nothing like this existed in the Soviet Union and its satellites, not even in the Kremlin's last days, nor in many of the other cases of successful nonviolent democratic revolution that have toppled so many tyrants in the past quarter century.

HOW TO DO IT

Iran is a classic case of what used to be known as a pre-revolutionary situation. The economy—insofar as it has to do with the daily lives of most people—is a disaster, the rulers are hated, the population is young, and there is a long tradition of self-government. So why hasn't there been a full-fledged revolution against the mullahs?

It's hard enough to figure out why something did happen, let alone why it didn't, but there are at least two important factors. The first is that revolutions rarely succeed without external support. Neither George Washington nor the Ayatollah Khomeini would have won without foreign help, nor would Lech Walesa in Poland, Corazon Aquino in the Philippnes, or Vaclav Havel in Czechoslovakia. Almost all contemporary revolutionary movements get help from someone outside, but Iran is a real oddity; so far as is known, not a single foreign government has been inclined to assist democratic revolution there.

The lack of an outside base of support goes hand in hand with a component of Iranian culture that is absolutely central to the chances of regime change: the Iranian people believe that major events, especially in their part of the world, only happen if the United States wants them to happen. Many Iranians will stay away from a revolutionary movement unless the American government openly and explicitly supports it. They need to hear the words from our leaders, then they need to see some palpable action.

The flip side of this belief in America's unique ability to influence their lives is that they are confident the regime will fall if the United States calls for it and acts to bring it down. In all probability, there would have been a massive uprising against the mullahs in the recent past—particularly in 2003, when the students and workers were gearing up for a general strike—if we had supported it. Instead, Secretary of State Powell went out of his way to announce we would do nothing to help the pro-democracy forces, which essentially shut down the plans for the uprising.

It is a mistake to think of "the opposition" as if it were a specific group of people; the opposition is made up of the overwhelming majority of the population. This suggests a winning scenario in which the regime, supported by an armed and relatively small number of loyalists, is confronted by huge numbers of peaceful demonstrators in every major city, against a background of near total paralysis of the country's key economic and social sectors: schools, factories, transportation, and the oil fields. How can the regime survive an insurrection by many millions of people?

It is often said that the regime and their fanatical security forces will fiercely fight to defend the Islamic Republic, and no doubt there are those who will want to fight. But it is one thing to fight against a few hundred or even a few thousand demonstrators; it is quite different—qualitatively different—to confront hundreds of thousands of well-organized people, calling for peaceful change. In one sense, this is a numbers game. If the revolution achieves critical mass, and the revolutionaries are prepared to fight—for the most part without using violence—the regime will not be able to impose its will.

There is already quite a large mass of dissidents, from women and students to ethnic minorities and Zoroastrians, workers and innumerable people at high levels of the regime, including grand ayatollahs such as Montazeri. It would take a separate book to recount the protests and demonstrations of the past few years, but it's easy to get the flavor of the revolutionary brew by looking at a few months in 2005, and then again in 2006–7.

Late in the spring of 2005, there were massive demonstrations and work stoppages in the oil-rich regions, centering around the city of Ahwaz. The demonstrators called for an end to the regime, scores of people were killed, and hundreds were beaten and arrested. On May Day, workers again demonstrated against the regime, this time in all the major cities. In Tehran, where the presidential election campaign was in full swing, strongman

Hashemi Rafsanjani was hooted down by the crowd, and pictures of him and Supreme Leader Khamenei were torn down and trampled.

As usual, there was no encouragement from Washington, but the protests went on. In October alone, there were protests at Najafabad and Abbasspour universities, an attack on governmental bureaus in the province of Qeshm in protest against the violent repression of peaceful demonstrations, a symbolic protest by bus drivers all over the country (they refused to validate passengers' tickets), a protest by dozens of women in Tehran against the unbearable social conditions in which they had to live, and a demonstration by hundreds of students at Beheshti University in Tehran, during which they set their dormitory on fire.

These are probably only a fraction of the actual agitation, since we only know of them from newspapers, broadcasts, and blogs. Many uprisings and protests are in areas not covered by foreign media, such as Baluchistan, Kurdistan, the Azeri regions, and the oil region of Khuzestan, heavily populated by Ahwazi Arabs, and we have only sporadic information from these areas.

The situation was further radicalized in 2006 and early 2007.

On January 28, 2006, some five hundred drivers, bus organization workers, and union organizers were arrested by the Iranian police after organizing a strike to protest the arrest and detention of Mansour Ossanlu, the head of the Union of Workers of the Tehran and Suburbs Bus Company. Photographs of Ossanlu following his subsequent release showed that his tongue had been sliced, and he had been beaten and burned.

In a long-standing pattern, workers all over Iran protested incredible delays in receiving their salaries, only to be beaten, arrested, and tortured. In September, hundreds of workers at the Alboz carpet workshops in Babol Sar protested because they hadn't been paid for nine months. They were beaten up by law enforcement forces. Later in the month, farmers in the Caspian village of Kamdarreh protested against the seizure of their land to build a new Islamic university. Security forces arrested two hundred and fifty of them at the protest and conducted house-to-house searches to locate others. Security forces then cut off water and electricity to the village. A local was quoted: "Not one man in sight . . . they've all been arrested or have fled to big cities or the nearby forests for fear of their lives. Most of their houses have been totally destroyed, forcing them to go to stay with relatives in neighboring villages. Now all financial responsibilities of the family are left on the shoulders of the women."

According to Agence France Presse in October 2006, close to two hundred thousand workers in five hundred factories had not received any salary for as much as fifty months. In January 2007, workers in Kohkiluyeh-Boyer Ahmadi-ye province brought families along to protest in front of the governor's office, demanding four years (!) of unpaid wages.

The students were even more aggressive, even as some of the best of them were struck down by the mullahs. Akbar Mohammadi, the brother of the founder of the independent student movement, died on July 31 in the Evin Prison. He died "suspiciously" during an eleven-day hunger strike, and his family subsequently showed photographs that demonstrated he had been savagely tortured. There was firsthand confirmation from his brother Manoucher, who had been in Evin Prison at the same time. The two brothers had been brought to the same room, so that they could watch each other undergo torture. Manoucher was given a one-day furlough to attend Akbar's funeral and fled the country. He crossed the border into Iraq, but was unable to obtain an American visa (his sister was attending college in California). Aware that he was being stalked by the Revolutionary Guards, he ran to Turkey. After several weeks he obtained a visa, but as he was about to board a plane in Istanbul for New York, he was arrested and jailed. Finally he was permitted to fly back to Iraq and subsequently reached the United States.

In late September, Amnesty International reported on

the deteriorating condition of Ahmad Batebi, citing a report written by his doctor. The doctor was then arrested.

In a widely reported event,[3] in December hundreds of
Iranian students confronted Ahmadinejad as he gave a
speech at Amirkabir University of Technology in Tehran.
They exploded firecrackers, called him a "fascist," and
burned pictures of him. There were cries of "Death to the
dictators." Ahmadinejad promised that no action would be
taken against the students, but in March fifty-four students were expelled, most of whom had participated in the
protests. The university chancellor then signed papers to
send the former students straight to the armed forces. The
expulsions and subsequent conscriptions followed further
student demonstrations at Alameh University, decrying
new disciplinary codes. The students brandished placards
protesting the "atmosphere of fascist control," and a female student said that if Ahmadinejad could take off the
brakes on Iran's nuclear program, the students could similarly release restraints on the fight for free speech and
progress.

As Radio Free Europe/Radio Liberty summarized the
situation at the beginning of 2007: "There was systematic
repression of free speech within the universities; students

---

[3] "Iran President Facing Revival of Students' Ire," *The New York
Times*, December 21, 2006.

were blackballed, suspended, and sometimes denied entry to graduate schools, and a number of student unions and newspapers were shut down."[4]

This was part of a broader clampdown, which started in the fall, on all Iranians who wanted greater freedom:

In addition to recent newspaper shutdowns—including leading reformist daily *Shargh*—the confiscation of satellite dishes and the arrests of outspoken journalists and intellectuals increased over the fall. The government also ordered Internet providers to reduce the bandwidth of residential and cybercafe service, making it harder for private citizens to access outside media sources. Kianoosh Sanjari was sent to Evin Prison for running a blog which chronicled the wave of detentions. . . . A recent film by Oscar-nominated director Bahman Ghobadi was also banned for depicting a woman singing.[5]

In addition, there were the ongoing efforts by Iranian women to gain equitable treatment from the regime, a cause that had been lost the day after the revolution. And finally, in early March, a monster teachers' demonstration.

---

[4] http://www.rfcrl.org/featuresarticle/2007/1/5BA5B5D4-C120-480A-87C1-563DC8043108.html.
[5] "Ahmadinejad's Autumn Crackdown on Free Speech," *Washington Times*, November 6, 2006.

Tens of thousands from thirty teachers' unions protested the mass firing of thousands of teachers (fifteen hundred in Kurdistan alone), threatening to call off midterm examinations and go on strike. Hundreds were arrested, but a few days later thousands more rallied in front of the parliament, demanding that the education minister be fired, their salaries increased, and their colleagues released and rehired. Security forces arrested key organizers in their homes and dragged them off to prison for interrogation, but demonstrations continued.

No objective observer can fail to recognize the explosiveness of the Iranian situation, the courage of the people, and the ongoing failure of the regime to achieve legitimacy in the people's eyes. The regime cracks down on the dissidents, but the protests continue.

The Iranian people need three things from us to catalyze their wide-ranging protests into an effective revolutionary force: hope, information, and some material support.

HOPE

Hope requires an explicit declaration that the United States wants regime change in Iran. It is not enough to say that we share their dream for freedom. We must say we want freedom for the Iranians. That means they must be free to choose their leaders, and their form of government.

To date, the Iranians feel they have been abandoned by the United States, and with good reason. In the spring of 2005, the Norouz celebrations described in the first chapter were put down by the usual regime thugs. The press reported modest demonstrations, but in fact they were much larger. According to Iranians with whom I spoke at the time, there were monster demonstrations in eleven provinces and thirty-seven cities, and many thousands of people—one source said more than thirty thousand—were arrested, some only briefly, others shipped off to the infamous prisons and torture chambers of the regime. The most dramatic events took place in Shiraz, where the demonstrators directed a chant toward Washington: "Bush, you told us to rise up, and so we have. Why don't you act?"

Which was precisely the right question. The president publicly promised the Iranian people that the United States would support them if they acted to win their own freedom, and the Iranians called on Bush to make good on that promise.

Hope requires a consistent message in support of the Iranian people from our officials and from our radios and televisions. The most important of these is the Voice of

America, which most Iranians believe represents the views of the American government. They are therefore often baffled to hear a parade of critics of American policy, and a remarkable number of defenders of the Iranian regime. This even applies to the nuclear question.

On April 18, 2006, for example, VOA Persian Service aired a special on Iran's nuclear program. The sole guest on the show's first segment was a Mr. Nakhai, whose professional affiliations were not presented to the listeners (he was an adviser to the Iranian regime). He predictably defended the Iranian performance and remarked that it was difficult for him to accept that the five permanent members of the UN Security Council, all of whom had "broken every rule of the Non-Proliferation Treaty, are sitting upon judgment of one country [Iran] that has obeyed every rule." No one on the show challenged this amazing statement.

This, alas, was typical VOA material. On March 14, 2006, VOA devoted an entire program and a segment of another to an op-ed from *The Washington Post* entitled "U.S. Push for Democracy Could Backfire Inside Iran," which was a critique of the administration's newly announced policy of promoting democratic civil society in Iran. Almost all the guests on the show agreed with the premise of the article.

The other main American transmission to Iran is Radio Farda, which broadcasts 65 percent pop music, and at most 1 percent news about Iran. Most of its nonmusic broadcasting is devoted to contemporary culture, not the life-and-death struggle for freedom in Iran.

Iranians can get plenty of music from commercial and other state broadcasts; official American radio and television should give them things they can't get elsewhere. We should, for example, broadcast interviews about Shi'ism, with particular attention to those several Shi'ite clerics in Najaf, Iraq, and elsewhere in the Middle East who strongly oppose the Khomeini worldview and the theocracy in Qom. Several Iraqi ayatollahs, including some who lived in Iran for many years, would love to do this, as would Khomeini's grandson Hossein Khomeini, who has openly criticized his grandfather's creation. And it is certainly possible to organize interviews with Ayatollahs Montazeri and Taheri, leading critics of the regime.

That sort of programming would demonstrate American concern for the future of the Shi'ite community and remind Iranians that the Islamic Republic's version of Shi'ism is only accepted by one-quarter of the world's Shi'ites.

The Bush administration has been consistently inattentive to the importance of broadcasting in the war against terror, while the Iranians excel at it. In Iraq, for example, we were shamefully unprepared to use radio and television to reach the Iraqi people, but the Iranians were ready from the get-go. As of May 15, 2003, none of Iraq's radio stations were on the air, but Iranian broadcasting was in full voice. SCIRI set up "the voice of the mujahideen" as soon as the war began and transmitted on the traditional frequency of the official Iranian state radio. The content was pure Iranian propaganda, aimed at inciting hatred of the United States, declaring America and Britain to be occupiers who had to be driven out, and proclaiming the coalition to be in league with "the Zionist entity."

It took the United States at least two full years before we were able to reach the full population of Iraq. We don't have that problem with Iran. We can reach them. But we often don't seem to know what we should say to them.

INFORMATION

We learned during the Cold War, in large part because of the extraordinary success of Radio Free Europe and Radio Liberty, that while it is relatively easy for oppressed peoples to get pretty good information about the world at large, it is damnably difficult for them to know what is going on inside their own country. American broadcasters accordingly devoted enormous attention to getting and broadcasting accurate information about events behind the Iron Curtain. The same applies to Iran; our radios and TVs have to constantly inform Iranians about *Iranian* news. People in Isfahan need to know what is happening in Tehran, Tabriz, and Shiraz, and vice versa. At the moment, VOA and Farda fail to broadcast very much information about Iran, noting the difficulty of getting reliable news and the virtual impossibility of having their own correspondents on the ground.

It's hard to take such objections seriously in a world of digital cameras embedded in cell phones, and near universal Internet access. If digital and video cameras were widely distributed, Iranians could send us photos and videos via e-mail, and we could then relay them throughout the country. Iranians have long since mastered the Internet (Farsi is said to be the fourth most popular online language), with innumerable Iranian bloggers incountry, and scores of them in the diaspora; they routinely provide information that no news organization could possibly get. In short, the information is there, and we should get it and broadcast it to a national audience.

The second important category of information is "how to do it," the "it" being democratic revolution. We should broadcast interviews with political leaders who have participated in successful democratic revolutions, so that the

Iranians get a solid grounding in the techniques of nonviolent conflict. They should hear from Poles, Czechs, Lebanese, Filipinos, Russians, etc., etc. What worked? What did *not* work? How do you gain the sympathy of the security forces?

Furthermore, case studies of successful nonviolent democratic revolutions are now on CDs and DVDs. They should be widely distributed and posted on blogs.

MATERIAL SUPPORT

During the Cold War, the fax machine was a revolutionary instrument. Today there are abundant such tools: satellite phones, laptops, servers, phone cards, software to beat the regime's "filtering" of the Internet, and so forth. Such material should be distributed to the key groups: students, teachers, workers (especially truck drivers and oil and textile workers), key religious leaders, both inside Iran and to their supporters outside.

The rationale for providing them with this technology is the same as broadcasting information: it enables the dissidents to be in touch with one another across the country. To that end, we should also support the best of the diaspora Persian-language broadcasters, most of whom are in Southern California, with a few others in

Europe and the Middle East. The mullahs recognize the importance of the foreign broadcasters. During several of the biggest demonstrations in Iran, people would call the California radio stations with up-to-date information, knowing that it would quickly be broadcast all over Iran. Once the regime figured it out, they spent a small fortune to jam the California broadcasts at difficult moments.

The "final days" for the regime are days of mass demonstrations and a shutdown of the country's productive enterprises. The latter requires large-scale strikes. To that end we need to encourage private enterprises and free trade-union organizations to build strike funds for the workers, so that they will be able to feed their families while they are on strike. This is a proven technique; Khomeini did it in the run-up to the Revolution, when he arranged to have millions of bags of rice sent to Iran (some of the bags also contained weapons).

Hope, information, and material support are the central ingredients of a strategy to support a nonviolent revolution in Iran. Several tactical questions remain, along with a few broader policy points.

First, given our decades of failure to challenge the Iranian regime, we should take steps to demonstrate that things have changed in Washington. The best way to do that is to appoint a special adviser to the president for Iranian affairs. That person should be someone the Iranians—regime and people alike—will instantly recognize as fully committed to regime change in Iran, who is knowledgeable about the country, and who is tough enough to win. That step alone will send a powerful message.

Second is the question about how best to support the revolutionaries. Should we do it openly or secretly? The answer to this important question should not be decided in Washington, because it should be their call, not ours. This is up to *them*. Our political and moral support will obviously be open. If they are happy to have it known that they are receiving telephones, DVDs, etc., from the United States, then we should just do it the most efficient way. But if, as is likely, the Iranians want at least some of it secret, we should certainly respect their wishes.

However it is done, it should not involve the CIA. Rightly or wrongly, many Iranians have lost confidence in the CIA, and they do not trust it to keep secrets. This was also true for many freedom fighters during the Cold War, and they greatly preferred to have contact with organizations such as the AFL-CIO. Unfortunately, that organization no longer plays a significant role in advancing the interests of free trade unions inside tyrannies, but similar groups do. Some of them would likely help Iranian dissidents get some of the material and money they need.

OBJECTIONS

There are three principal arguments against this course of action:

- Revolution cannot succeed in Iran because the repression is too powerful and resolute, and because there is no effective leader inside the country (and if one emerged, the mullahs would kill him).
- You can't bring down this regime with nonviolent means, the mullahs have no remorse about arresting, killing, and torturing large numbers of people. Hence the insurrection will have to be armed, and we may have to use military power to support them.
- The major issue today is Iran's nuclear program, and a revolution can't happen fast enough. Hence we may have to use military power.

To which there is a fourth objection, having to do with Washington: how can anyone expect this president and this administration to do anything as ambitious as supporting revolution in Iran when they have failed to do any such thing in more than six years in office?

These are all serious objections, and they have publicly been advanced by thoughtful people. I think they are overstated. Remember that Machiavelli reminds us that tyranny is the most unstable form of government. I believe the Islamic Republic is highly unstable and essentially hollow, with little popular support, and a coterie of camp followers who are ready to jump ship with minimal encouragement. The recent wave of defections at high levels of the Revolutionary Guards testifies to that. We were amazed at the speed with which the Soviet empire collapsed, and I expect the Iranian regime would similarly collapse at an epic rate.

We defeated the Soviet empire at a time when only a small minority of its people were willing to fight for freedom. We overthrew Milosevic with a minority of the Yugoslavs. Syrian domination over Lebanon was defeated with a minority of the Lebanese. In Iran we have upward of 70 percent of the people on our side. If we supported them, I think it quite likely that we could liberate Iran in less than a year. Is that fast enough? I hope so, although nobody really knows how close they are to the bomb.

The Soviet Union had vast instruments of repression (the KGB was legendary, and it was said that 40 percent of the people were in their employ, one way or another) and was every bit as ruthless as the mullahs. Yet it imploded. Violence was not necessary, and we certainly did not need to use military power to bring it down. Why should we not work for the same outcome in Iran?

The question of leadership is probably less daunting than it appears. It is quite true that no single unifying figure is inside the country today, and it is a lot more difficult for overseas Iranians to lead a revolution than it was at the time of the shah. The mullahs learned that lesson. One after another, potential revolutionary leaders have been murdered or incarcerated, and under current conditions no national opposition figure calling for regime change could survive. But that does not mean they don't exist; it only means we don't know their names and faces. There is so much opposition to the regime, and there is so much political talent in Iran, that such leaders must surely exist. I rather suspect that the real problem will prove to be a surfeit of good leaders, rather than a shortage.

In any event, the most serious objection is not about capable Iranian leaders, but American ones. President Bush is in many ways a mystery. His many speeches and press conferences demonstrate that he has well understood the peril of Iran, and the importance of supporting freedom in the region. For many years, half the world expected he would insist that we actively endorse regime change in Iran, but he has not. Time is running out on his presidency. Will he yet do what his words have always implied? It seems unlikely, but then human history is full of surprises, and strong support for the Iranian people would be decidedly more consistent with Bush's words than the strange inaction that has characterized his policy to date.

Then there are the military options. The first is to use military power to destroy, or at least effectively damage, Iran's nuclear program, while the second is more ambitious, to use military power as the primary instrument of regime change. The first would most likely be launched at the "eleventh hour," based on the certainty that the mullahs were on the verge of having atomic bombs and/or nuclear-tipped ballistic missiles. It's unlikely that we will have the necessary degree of certainty, and this administration's unhappy experience with the CIA's assessment of the Iraqi WMD program suggests that we will probably not soon go to war based on an intelligence assessment.

The second military option—to bring down the regime by bombing it (nobody advocates a large-scale invasion)—is one of those "scenarios" that has to be evaluated, even if the odds of it ever happening are prohibitively long. Several distinguished theoreticians of airpower believe that a modern state can be dismantled with today's smart weapons, and they sometimes argue that a sufficiently intelligent choice of targets can deliver a political message to the people and thereby stimulate revolution. There is some anecdotal Iranian support for this theory. It is said that when we were liberating Afghanistan, some Iranians held up banners on their side of the border saying, "Bomb here please." And in the days following the defenestration of Saddam Hussein, the French daily *Le Monde* had a female journalist in Tehran interview Iranians and ask them what they thought about all those U.S. marines running around Baghdad. Almost all the Iranians said, in essence, "Why are they only in Baghdad? We could use some marines here."

Needless to say, such anecdotes are not a guide for good policy, and while a military attack could stimulate a mass uprising, it could also provoke an eruption of anti-Americanism along the lines of "first they abandon us, now they bomb us." Nobody knows, and indeed it is probably unknowable. But military action becomes more likely with the passage of time (as the mullahs' crash nuclear program advances) and without an effective policy of regime change. If, in the end, an American president orders an attack on Iran, it will be terrible testimony to the failure of this country to deal effectively with the Islamic Republic from the moment of its violent creation.

Finally, the broader policy question. We cannot possibly "win" in Iraq and Afghanistan alone, because Iraq and

Afghanistan are single battlefields in a (at a mininum) regional war. The Iranians, Syrians, and (a significant group of) Saudis dare not acquiesce in the creation of a free and successful Iraq because that would mortally threaten their own survival. The regimes in Tehran, Damascus, and Riyadh are extremely unpopular; their peoples are aching for the chance to remove the regimes and experiment with freedom. The regimes know that and are ruthlessly oppressing their peoples at the same time they are supporting the terrorists in Iraq, hoping to drive us out of the region and thereby sit more comfortably on their thrones.

Iran is the key to this war, as it has been from the beginning. If the mullahs retain power in Tehran, we are truly in for a long war, possibly a nuclear war. If they fall, the world will change overnight. Put yourself for a moment in the tight shoes of Iraqi prime minister Maliki. He comes from the Shi'ite underground, a terrorist organization. He knows—in spades—the ability of Iranian intelligence agents to assassinate anyone deemed an enemy. He sees—in detail—that the Iranians are all over his country, killing his people, killing Americans and Brits. His very life depends on his ability to navigate the tricky waters of the vast Middle East war. He knows the Americans put him in office, and so he's got to find a way to make them happy, but he also knows the Iranians can remove him from the world of the living. He's got to make them happy, too. They want an Islamic Republic, which is counter to the wishes of the Iraqi Shi'ite leaders, and probably to his own desires. What to do?

It all depends on whether we can defeat the mullahs. If Maliki thought we were going to win the Middle East war, he'd be our best friend. But he has no reason to believe that. Thus far, we have given the Iranians (and the Syrians) a free shot at Iraq. After all, only in late 2006 did we even authorize American troops to shoot or capture Iranians in Iraq. If a man like Maliki—and this analysis applies to all the other leaders of the region—does not see clear signs that we have the will to bring down the mullahs, then he will make a cold-blooded calculation: the Americans will leave in the foreseeable future, and the mullahs will still be there. His survival will then in large part depend on them.

We can win this thing, if we will fight the real war in the most effective way, using our most potent weapons. Bernard Lewis has the final words, delivered at the American Enterprise Institute's annual banquet in March 2007: "The idea of freedom in its Western interpretation is making headway. It is becoming more and more understood, more and more appreciated, and more and more desired. It is perhaps in the long run our best hope, perhaps even our only hope, of surviving this developing struggle."

EPILOGUE:
A FINAL LOOK IN
EARLY SUMMER

The danger of the past was that men became slaves. The danger of the future is that men may become robots.

—Erich Fromm

M ost of this book was written in the spring of 2007, and copyedited in April. This final section was written in the first week of June, by which time the United States and Iran had held formal talks about Iraq in Baghdad, the Iranian leaders had reiterated their refusal to terminate or suspend the enrichment of uranium, and new evidence had emerged to further document the material in previous chapters. Domestic repression had gotten even worse, particularly against women, the wreckage of the economy continued apace, and proof of Iranian support for both Shi'ite and Sunni terrorists in the Middle East had become more abundant. No policy change had taken place.

By early June 2007, both Iranians and Americans were pursuing their dreams with heightened intensity. Despite nearly thirty years of evidence that no such strategy could work, the Americans, led by Secretary of State Condoleezza Rice and her right-hand man, Under Secretary R. Nicholas Burns, were firmly committed to a "diplomatic solution." The Iranians, encouraged by voices from Congress in Washington calling for a speedy withdrawal of American armed forces from Iraq, pressed forward rapidly on multiple fronts, operating against their enemies in the Middle East and in the West, including America. Ahmadinejad announced at the beginning of June that the "final countdown" had begun for Israel, and called upon Lebanese and Palestinian forces (both of whom were receiving considerable Iranian assistance) to destroy the Jewish state.[1] Meanwhile, in May, the Islamic Republic took American hostages in Iran. The five American hostages were:

---

[1] "Ahmadinejad says clock ticking to Israel's 'destruction'," *Yahoo News*, June 3, 2007.

- Haleh Esfandiari, the director of the Middle East program at the Woodrow Wilson Center in Washington and the wife of the distinguished historian Shaul Bakash;
- Parnaz Azima, a journalist for Radio Farda, the Farsi-language component of Radio Free Europe/Radio Liberty;
- Ali Shakeri, a founding board member at the University of California, Irvine's, Center for Citizen Peacebuilding;
- Kian Tajbakhsh, a consultant working for George Soros's Open Society Institute; and
- Robert A. Levinson, a former FBI officer reportedly investigating tobacco smuggling on behalf of a private client. He disappeared after he flew to Iran's Kish Island in March.

The two women—Esfandiari and Azima—were regular visitors to Iran, and both were visiting their mothers at the time of their arrests.

Iranian and Iranian-supported terrorists had been trying unsuccessfully to capture Americans in Iraq for some time. In September 2006, for example, a mixed American-Iraqi force was patrolling the Iranian border. According to an official Army summary of the event, dated September

7, from the 101st Airborne Division, a U.S. Cavalry group patrolling the Iran/Iraq border with six Iraqis came across a couple of Iranian soldiers on the Iraqi side of the border. When the Iranians saw them, they jumped back into Iran. Later, "the patrol came upon a single Iranian soldier on the Iraqi side of the border who did not flee." So the joint patrol engaged the Iranian in conversation (at that time, the rules of engagement did not permit us to shoot or arrest the Iranians). Suddenly, an Iranian platoon appeared, and surrounded the Americans. The Iranian commander informed the joint patrol that "if they tried to leave their location the Iranians would fire upon them," and indeed members of the Iranian group opened fire with small arms and rocket-propelled grenades. The Iraqis, who were obviously in cahoots with the Iranians, quietly walked away. The American in charge—a young Army captain—immediately ordered his men to attack. Several Iranians were killed, and the Americans escaped. The Iranians kept on firing but didn't hit anyone.

The Iranians would no doubt have preferred to kidnap American soldiers, but such events seemed to convince them to go after softer targets. The actual victims could not have been easier: four of the five were Iranian-American civilians within Iranian borders (the Islamic Republic not recognizing dual citizenship, the hostages were considered Iranian, and subject to the whims of the regime). At least two of them were charged with espionage, and Ms. Esfandiari was accused of an additional crime: being married to a Jew. In the words of a Web site closely tied to President Ahmadinejad, Ms. Esfandiari is "married to Shaul Bakhash, a Jew, [and] is one of the leading figures in the international Zionist lobby planning the overthrow of the Iranian regime, including the Zionist regime's plans to attack Iran."[2]

Actually, Ms. Esfandiari was one of the leading figures in the intellectual/scholarly opposition to the Bush Administration, Ms. Azima worked for an organization that has been a feckless voice of confusion and a frequent critic of American policy in the Middle East, and Messrs. Tajbakhsh and Shakeri are advocates of dialogue with Iran. I don't know anything about Mr. Levinson's politics or religion. Not that the actual views of the hostages had anything to do with their plight; they were taken hostage because they were American citizens.

The latest hostage crisis was initiated for the same reasons the regime has so often taken foreign hostages, beginning in the first year of its existence: to resolve internal

---

[2] http://www.iran-press-service.com/ips/articles-2007/may2007/esfandiari-arrested-10507.shtml.

power struggles, to convince the Iranian people of the hopelessness of their condition by directly challenging the infidels to do anything about it, and to impose their will on a Western world the mullahs view as feckless and paralyzed. When the American Embassy was overrun in the fall of 1979, Khomeini famously proclaimed that America "can't do a damn thing,"[3] and this past spring, the regime was once again trying to show that neither the Americans nor the Brits (five more of whom were taken hostage in Baghdad in March) could do anything to challenge the mullahcracy.

THE INTERNAL POWER STRUGGLE

The Supreme Leader, Ayatollah Ali Khamenei, was in the agonies of inoperable cancer and had already outlived his doctors' prognosis. The political war over his successor had been raging for several months between partisans of the country's two most prominent political figures, President Ahmadinejad and former president Hashemi Rafsanjani. In the spring, Rafsanjani had gone to Qom, the city of the grand ayatollahs, in an attempt to gain the support of the leading clerics, and trying to convince them to name a

---

[3] "The Exodus," *Iran Shahr*, July 1, 2005.

successor even before the Supreme Leader's demise. Nothing came of it, nor did anything come of the much-ballyhooed efforts to "impeach" Ahmadinejad or shorten his term. The latest dustup came over the Memorial Day talks with the Americans in Baghdad, which were violently condemned by Ahmadinejad's followers. The wave of hostage-taking undoubtedly played a role in this political war, for it demonstrated the great strength of the hardliners around Ahmadinejad and Khamenei, and weakened Rafsanjani's standing with the clerical elite.

THE MESSAGE TO THE IRANIAN PEOPLE

Two of the American hostages—Esfandiari and Tajbakhsh—were charged with attempting to subvert the Islamic Republic and organize a "soft revolution" against the regime. At the same time, the mullahs launched a new wave of political repression against students, teachers, women, intellectuals and, most recently, scientists. The Information Ministry, a.k.a. the secret intelligence service, warned that any Iranian who attended overseas conferences would automatically fall under suspicion of cooperating with foreign espionage operations.[4] All these

---

[4] "Iran Spying Chief Warns Academics," *BBC News*, May 30, 2007.

measures are symptomatic of a regime that knows it is hated by most Iranians, and therefore fears a popular uprising.

The mullahs constantly seek to demonstrate that America is impotent, thus hoping to discourage potential challenges from below. What better way than to take American (and British) hostages, and show that the United States (and Her Majesty's Government) are powerless to do anything about it?

THE WAR AGAINST THE INFIDELS

Finally, there was the nearly thirty-year old ongoing war against America, which the mullahs firmly believed they were winning. They were supremely confident that the United States would be driven out of Iraq—largely by terrorists armed, funded, trained, and guided by Tehran—by the end of Bush's tenure. They were similarly optimistic about Afghanistan, where the Karzai Government and NATO military officers had become increasingly outspoken about Iran's role in arming both the Taliban and terrorists associated with Gulbuddin Hekmatyar. Indeed, the Iranian hand was manifest in lethal activities from Afghanistan to Lebanon, Iraq, and Gaza. The capture of American hostages was an integral part of

that strategy, aiming blow after blow against the perceived tottering giant whose fall would open the flood-
gates of jihad against the infidel West. It was rather like
the picadors lancing the bull's body to weaken it, thereby
facilitating the matador's fatal thrust.

In other words, the most recent developments confirmed the tyrannical nature of the regime, the explosive
internal dynamics of the country, and the grim determination of the mullahs to destroy the West.

THE FUTURE OF THE REGIME

The nature of the regime is best demonstrated by its
treatment of women, who constitute the best-educated
segment of the population and who have shown excep-
tional tenacity in their fight for justice. The mullahs' hy-
persensitivity to women's activities ranged from the
ridiculous to the sublime, but there is little room for
common sense in a worldview that sees women's hair as
the source of emanations of dangerous sexual energy that
corrupt otherwise virtuous men. The Ayatollah Khomeini reserved some of his strongest condemnations for the
Shah's practice of permitting women to teach male students, and just last year, when President Ahmadinejad
proposed to admit women to soccer games (to be sure, in

segregated areas of the stadium), he was quickly slapped down by the Supreme Leader.[5]

Indeed, the Islamic Republic recently cancelled an agreement that would have sent the national women's soccer team to Germany to play the second leg of a home-and-home contest against a multicultural team in Berlin.[6] In April 2006, BSV Aldersimspor, whose players come from Turkish, German, Korean, Greek, and Tunisian backgrounds, had gone to Tehran for the first match (which ended in a tie). It was the first time the Iranian team had played against a foreign team in a real stadium with spectators, all women of course. The Iranians imposed the dress code—all players were forced to wear special head scarves—and everything went off without a hitch.

The rematch was scheduled for Berlin, June 8, but the Iranians postponed it at the last minute. Was it because there would be men in the stadium? Because the German team members would not have their hair covered? Because protests were planned to support the plight of Iranian women? Probably all these factors played a role, but the underlying motive was undoubtedly the conviction that any license granted to Iranian women was danger-

---

[5] "Iran's Women Barred from Soccer Games," *USA Today*, May 8, 2006.
[6] http://www.spiegel.de/international/germany/0,1518,druck-48608 6,00.html.

ous, especially in an international setting that might generate foreign support for women's causes back home.

Back home, women's causes were indeed gaining international attention and domestic support, and thus encountering harsher repression. *Der Spiegel* covered the story in mid-May,[7] writing of the "burgeoning feminist movement" and the regime's actions to crush it. Ironically, "even as the world has taken little notice of the activists, Iranian authorities have." The crackdown came despite the feminists' decision to tone down their protests, concentrating on gathering signatures for petitions to change the country's anti-female laws. It didn't work; one of the leading campaigners for women's rights, Zeinab Peyghambarzadeh, was arrested in early May, leading one of her allies, Jila Banlyaghoub, to tell foreign reporters that the regime was "warning . . . that they will not tolerate even the mildest criticism."

The regime's crackdown was not just aimed against feminist activists, but against women in general. The moral police increased their harassment of insufficiently modest clothing, rounding up scores of women, dragging them off to prison, and forcing them into chadors.[8] And

---

[7] "Tehran Cracks Down on Feminist Movement," *Der Spiegel*, May 17, 2007.
[8] "Tehran Police Clashes with Women," *roozonline*, May 26, 2007.

a new quota system was drafted for the university population, limiting women to half the slots available, instead of the 65 percent they actually hold.[9]

The narrowing of opportunity for Iranian women in higher education was more a symbolic blow than a real one, for the country's general degradation had produced a dramatic shrinking of the labor market, including university graduates. According to a detailed analysis from the *Iran Analytical Report*, "many young men and women now . . . opt out of higher education because it does not translate into a good job." In fact, according to the same study, "a majority of graduates end up doing unskilled work or migrating overseas."[10] And things were just as bad on the other side of the lecture hall; teachers' salaries were unconscionably low, and infrequently paid, provoking constant strikes and protests against the regime.

The mounting social misery made President Ahmadinejad the target of Iranian frustration and rage. He had come to office as the self-proclaimed protector of the downtrodden, and he presided over the militarization of the Iranian bureaucracy, placing his comrades from the Revolutionary Guards in every important government

---

[9] "Iran: Conservatives Draft Legislation to Limit Women's Access to University," *Adnkronos International*, January 26, 2007.

[10] "Iran's Workforce in Disarray," *Iran Analytical Report* (Washington, D.C.), May 15, 2007.

office down several levels. This was entirely in harmony with the Supreme Leader's decision to clamp down on the Iranian people, and the presence of military personnel in so many key positions made the regime's iron fist dramatically visible.

Despite his promise to improve the lot of the common people, and bring greater discipline to Iranian society, Ahmadinejad's new government brought neither greater order nor greater material comfort, even though everybody knew that the surge in oil prices initially provided a huge influx of cash. Whatever fraction of the oil bonanza was allocated to public works and social welfare (the lion's share undoubtedly went for support of terrorism and military programs), it was quickly consumed, forcing the government to tap into the Strategic Reserve Fund. This in turn undermined the value of the currency, and unleashed a wave of inflation, further pauperizing the society. Khamenei tried to remedy the situation by promising to privatize state-owned enterprises by distributing 80 percent of the shares to the people, but most of the shares in successful companies have been sold to regime favorites, especially members of the Revolutionary Guards and the Basij forces, while the poor have only been able to buy into bankrupt companies, many of which have been shut down, and their employees driven onto the dole.

Things are equally bad for the workers, whether employed or not. As labor leaders such as the bus drivers' Mansour Osanloo has been at pains to point out, despite workers' protections in the Constitution, the Islamic Republic has passed laws that effectively deprive them of any meaningful rights. In practice, employers can exercise an option to simply declare their workers "temporary," and lay them off. Worse yet, it is very difficult to create workers' organizations, and those that do exist are strictly regulated by the regime. The final nail in the coffin is that employers regularly "delay" payment of unemployment benefits to their ex-workers.

The failures of the regime inevitably redounded against the president and his men, since Ahmadinejad had left no doubt about his own personal responsibility: most of his economic policies have been enacted by executive order, instead of due deliberation in Parliament. The economic failures have thus been blamed on him, and, having cut out the elected politicians in the Majlis, and having ostentatiously staffed out the government with his own military people, he has seriously undermined his base of popular support.

As the *Iran Analytical Report* concludes, "the lack of peaceful options for change has created a dangerous situation for the regime. The very people that the Islamic Republic swore to protect are disillusioned and resentful.

If nothing is done soon, this may be the greatest threat to the country's survival."[11]

The regime is acutely aware of the rage of the Iranian people, which it goes to such extremes to crush. The explosive anger of the Iranians constitutes one of the several timers clicking away the hours leading up to the likely wave of violence that will define the future of the region, and much of the rest of the world. Another is in Washington, a third is in Iraq, and the fourth is around Israel, from Gaza and the Palestinian Authority to Lebanon and Syria. If the Islamic Republic can drive the United States out of Iraq, destroy the fledgling democracy in Lebanon, and damage or destroy Israel, the mullahs believe they can dominate the area, including their own people. If they are seen to fail, however, their destiny is uncertain. That is why they are pushing so hard on all fronts, hoping to score their own victories before they fall. It is also why they are given to so much bluster, chest-pounding, and bellicose threats, as they try to buy more time for their schemes to succeed.

But time is not necessarily working in their favor. Like us, they face considerable internal opposition. Unlike us, their domestic opponents wish to end the very nature of their government, and create one that resembles ours. If

---

[11] http://www.iranreport.org/Weeklies/05-15-2007.htm.

the critics of American policy prevail in Washington, they will not immediately banish all members of the old order to an unhappy destiny. The mullahs know this, and seek victory as quickly as possible. All of which explains why the Iranian role in Iraq, Syria, Lebanon, and Gaza, so long brilliantly hidden in the fog of the regional war, has recently become so luminously clear. The urgency of their situation compels the mullahs to act in haste, and, contrary to much of the conventional wisdom, many things are going badly for them on the battlefields of the Middle East.

THE WAR

On January 20, 2007, twelve terrorists disguised as American military personnel entered the Provincial Joint Coordination Center in Karbala, where U.S. soldiers were meeting with local officials. It was clear from the way the operation was carried out that it had been carefully rehearsed. According to a subsequent report,[12] "The attackers went straight to where Americans were located in the provincial government facility, bypassing

---

[12] http://billroggio.com/archives/2007/01/the_karbala_attack_a.php.

the Iraqi police in the compound." Four American soldiers were handcuffed, taken away, and executed. Three others were wounded and another killed by a grenade thrown into the Karbala offices during the attack. Another two, handcuffed together, were found alive in a truck.

American analysts were confident that the Iranians were involved, because of the great sophistication of the terrorist unit. The terrorists needed to act as if they were Americans (for all we know, all or some of them may have actually been Americans), they needed to accumulate considerable material, from the uniforms and military vehicles to the weapons and radios. Moreover, it was a replay of a Hezbollah operation conducted against the Israelis along the Lebanese border the previous summer. That operation was known to have been conducted personally by Imad Mughniyah, the longtime master of Hezbollah operations, the same man who had designed and commanded the bombing of the U.S. and French Marine barracks in Lebanon twenty-four years earlier.

The American assessment proved correct. In a manhunt in Iraq for Sheikh Azhar al-Dulaymi (the leader of the group that actually conducted the Karbala massacre), U.S. special forces captured internal documents that showed that Dulaymi had been trained by Hezbollah and received assistance from the IRGC.[13] The manhunt eventually led to Dulaymi himself, who was killed in May on a rooftop in the Sadr City neighborhood of Baghdad. Rowan Scarborough, who reported the discovery of the documents, noted that "the direct involvement of Tehran's agents and Hezbollah in Dulaymi's terrorist cell indicates a deeper Iranian involvement than previously known."

The evidence did not stop there; we obtained additional information linking Iran to the Karbala attack.[14] In May, Major General William Caldwell announced that "we know they had built a mock facility in Iran and, in fact, it helped conduct the training and planning over there before they came back and executed that here in Iraq." This, too, was part of Hezbollah's standard operating procedure; the Iranians had built models of the American and French barracks in Lebanon in 1983 in order to train Mughniyah's operatives for the suicide bombings.

As before, evidence mounted to demonstrate the considerable support for Sunni terrorists coming from the Islamic Republic. As Simon Tisdall wrote in *The Guardian* in May:

---

[13] *Cf.* The report by Rowan Scarborough in *The Examiner* (Washington, D.C.), May 21, 2007, p. 1.
[14] http://edition.cnn.com/2007/WORLD/meast/05/25/iraq.iran/index.html.

Tehran's strategy . . . is national in scope and not confined to the Shia south, its traditional sphere of influence. . . . It included stepped-up coordination with Shia militias such as Moqtada al-Sadr's Jaish al-Mahdi as well as Syrian-backed Sunni Arab groups and al-Qaida in Mesopotamia, he added. Iran was also expanding contacts across the board with paramilitary forces and political groups, including Kurdish parties such as the PUK, a US ally.[15]

This information came from a senior American military officer in Baghdad, and shows two things: the willingness of our men in the field to finally come forward with the damning information about Iran (information of a sort that had been available for years), and the urgency with which the Iranians were ordering the terror network into action against us. As of late April, General David Petraeus, the American commander in Iraq, was speaking openly about our knowledge of Iranian-sponsored terrorist cells, and the success of American ground operations against the network of "secret cells" showed that the information was reliable. Between April 27 and June 7, twenty-five terrorists were killed and sixty-eight captured. Here is the sequence:[16]

---

[15] Simon Tisdall in *The Guardian* (London, May 22, 2007).
[16] http://billroggio.com/archives/2007/06/targeting_the_irania.php.

April 26: General Petraeus briefed on the capture of members of the Qazali and Sheibani networks.

April 27: Four captured during a raid in Sadr City.

May 3: Two captured during raids in Sadr City.

May 4: Sixteen captured during a raid in Sadr City, and a large Iranian supplied weapons cache found south of Baghdad.

May 6: Ten killed during a raid against a Sadr City "torture room," which also led to the discovery of a large weapons cache.

May 10: Four captured, 3 killed during raids in Sadr City.

May 13: Three captured during a raid in Sadr City.

May 19: Six captured, one killed during raids in northeast Baghdad. Azhar al-Dulaimi, the "mastermind" and "tactical commander" of the Karbala attack and a leader in the Qazali network was the man killed.

May 25: One captured, four killed in Raids in Basra and Sadr City. "The individual targeted [in Sadr City] is suspected of having direct ties to the leader of the EFP network as well as acting as a proxy for an Iranian Revolutionary Guard Corps officer." "The British killed Abu Qader, the leader of the Mahdi Army in Basra, along with his brother and two aides."

May 26: One captured, five killed during raids in Sadr City. "The individual detained during the raid is believed to be the suspected leader in a secret cell terrorist network . . ."

May 27: One captured during a raid in Sadr City.

May 30: Six captured during a raid in Sadr City, including one cell leader.

May 31: Two captured during a raid in Sadr City.

June 5: Six captured, one killed during two raids in Baghdad. One of those captured "is an integral member of the improvised explosive devises and EFP facilitation network . . . also believed to be responsible for numerous attacks against Coalition Forces, including heavy involvement in mortar attacks, personally observing and adjusting fire in the past two days."

June 7: Sixteen captured during a raid in Sadr City.

To further nail down the case against the mullahs, during a raid in late May, we captured a "liaison to al

Qaeda in Iraq senior leaders, who assists in the movement of information and documents from al Qaeda in Iraq leadership in Baghdad to al Qaeda senior leaders in Iran."[17]

The Intelligence Community let it be known to favored journalists that we actually had lots of inside information on Iranian activities, telling *Newsweek* about a shadowy, supersecret group inside the Quds Force that "acts as a liaison between the insurgents and the Revolutionary Guards," precisely what had been discovered by Coalition forces during the raid in late May. And the Intelligence informers conceded that Iran has "even begun to help Sunni insurgent groups."[18]

Meanwhile, in the horn of Africa, the president of Somalia's transitional government accused the Pakistani, Iranian, and unnamed Arab governments, of sponsoring a terror war against his administration, while across the Islamic Republic's eastern border, NATO announced that the Iranians had been caught providing weapons to yet another group widely believed to be ideologically incompatible with the mullahs: the Afghan Taliban.[19]

---

[17] Bill Roggio, *The Fourth Rail*, May 31, 2007.
[18] Mark Hosenball in "Periscope," *Newsweek*, June 4, 2007.
[19] The first report, of many, was by *ABC News:* http://blogs.abcnews .com/theblotter/2007/06/document_iran_c.html.

NATO officials say they have caught Iran red-handed, shipping heavy arms, C4 explosives, and advanced roadside bombs to the Taliban for use against NATO forces, in what the officials say is a dramatic escalation of Iran's proxy war against the United States and Great Britain. "It is inconceivable that it is anyone other than the Iranian government that's doing it," said former White House counterterrorism official Richard Clarke, an ABC News consultant.

As usual, top Bush Adminstration officials struggled bravely to maintain the fiction that we had no "hard information" proving the involvement of the Iranian leaders, but an assessment written by "a senior coalition official" stated flatly that "this is part of a considered policy, rather than the result of low-level corruption and weapons smuggling."

Nonetheless, the self-deception of the past three decades continues to entrance our diplomats. Secretary of Defense Robert Gates reiterated the mantra that we do not definitively know if the Iranian leaders have personally approved the support of terrorists throughout the region; we only know that the support comes from Iran. This is unworthy of Mr. Gates, who was one of the most brilliant analysts in the Intelligence Community. He knows what his commanders on the ground know, that in a dictatorship like the Islamic Republic, such large-scale assistance to terrorists is impossible without a green light from the Supreme Leader himself. No basic strategic decision can be made without his okay.

The Secretary of State granted that Iran was up to no good, but insisted[20] that it should not get in the way of negotiating with the mullahs over their nuclear program and their murderous meddling in Iraq.

> Iran's detention of at least four Americans is not a new hostage crisis akin to the seizure of U.S. diplomats three decades ago, Secretary of State Condoleezza Rice said . . . the top U.S. diplomat said the detentions are unwarranted but will not stop the United States from trying to engage Iran on other matters, including its disputed nuclear program and alleged support of insurgents in Iraq. "Let's not try to go back to an historical analogy that I think is a very different set of circumstances," Rice said of comparisons to the 1979 hostage standoff. After all, "(the hostages) are not linked up with what we are doing in other" forums.

As in the past, such statements reinforce the mullahs' conviction that our will is weak, and that they can do any-

---

[20] Anne Gearan and Matthew Lee, "Rice Interview: No Iran Hostage Crisis," Associated Press, June 8, 2007.

thing they wish without fear of reprisal. The diplomats no doubt believe they are doing everything possible to avoid a bloody confrontation with Iran, but the opposite is true. By refusing to challenge the mullahs, they encourage bloodshed, including that of our own people.

REVOLUTION

In like manner, a strategy of regime change—written off as utopian by the self-proclaimed realists—offers a chance for success. Those of us who advocate democratic revolution are often criticized for an excess of naiveté, for failing to recognize that the passion for freedom is not universal, and that there are many people—perhaps even many peoples and the followers of some religions—who despise democracy. Given half a chance, the realists say, much of the world will choose tyranny.

It is certainly true, but only up to a point. Students of fascism have long noted the enormous, near-total enthusiasm with which it was embraced by its followers, who came from very advanced cultures and had plenty of experience with self-government. Italy and Germany were among the most cultured, civilized, and humane countries on the face of the earth. But all that culture proved useless against the onslaught of the totalitarian mass movements. For most of the fascist era there was no real sign that the German or Italian people had serious second thoughts about living under tyranny, no real resistance worthy of the name . . . until the dictators began to lose the war, which changed everything. Hitler and Mussolini gained political power in traditional political ways, were reelected with enormous mandates, and governed without much in the way of opposition until they were finally done in by Allied armies, the greatest instruments of freedom in the twentieth century.

When people say, as they often do, with a glint of ethnic or cultural superiority in their angry eyes, that Arabs or Africans or Persians or Turks just aren't "ready" for democracy, that such people prefer tyrants, or that they have no history of democracy and are hence incapable of it, or they have no middle class, without which no stable democracy can exist, or they believe in Islam, which brooks no democracy, they need to be reminded that some of the worst tyrannies came from highly cultured Christian countries with glorious democratic and humanistic traditions, and active middle classes. Fascism was born in the land of Dante, Michelangelo, and Galileo and quickly spread to the countries of Goethe, Beethoven, and Freud. Those who argue that a phenomenon like Islamic fascism is just one more symptom of a "failed society," or of a backward culture or a hateful religion, seem not to know that fascism came from the most refined cultures in the world.

Further, it's silly to believe that a society without democratic traditions can't create a democracy; if that were true, there would never have been any democracies at all. Every democratic country was once a tyranny.

The horror of fascism—in many ways the real model for today's terror masters—is precisely its popular success. It's not just that people accept it, or endure it; they embrace it and celebrate it. Today's Islamic fascism is very much in that tradition. Other intellectual conceits contribute to our lack of understanding of our current enemy, and of the most potent weapons at our disposal. It's not easy for some modern thinkers to accept the true nature of the Islamic fascists, because of the long-discredited but still popular theory that revolutions are invariably a good thing, a righteous eruption against social and economic misery inflicted by greedy oppressive governments. In that view, revolutions are signs of progress, another step along the road to modernity.

But, especially in the twentieth century, many important revolutions were reactionary outbursts against modernity, a desperate attempt to restore an earlier (and often imaginary) style of politics in which the state, or the leader, made most of the fundamental decisions, thereby sparing the citizens the many agonizing choices that afflict modern man. One of the greatest thinkers to grapple with these issues was Erich Fromm, who explained in *Escape from Freedom* that totalitarian mass movements helped modern man escape from the awesome burdens of freedom, and then later argued that such mass movements fulfilled a collective death wish, a sort of epidemic of political necrophilia. Fromm is an invaluable guide to much of what is going on in the Middle East today.

When the Iranians overthrew the Shah twenty-eight years ago, it was fashionable in the West to hail the revolution and to "explain" it as an explosion of freedom against a tyrannical dictator. But it was the opposite; it was the sort of pathology that Fromm understood. Khomeini's attack on the Shah was not that the Shah was insufficiently modern and liberal, but rather too modern, too tolerant, too progressive. Khomeini promised to turn back the clock, not advance it; there would be less freedom for women and for infidels, and medieval methods of "justice," like stoning to death, would be reinstated. Khomeini offered the Iranians a chance to link their anger at the Shah with their terrible fear of freedom.

To be sure, many of Khomeini's supporters deluded themselves into believing that his promises were just rhetoric. Others hoped that, once in power, he would "moderate." But he didn't. He plunged Iran into a new Dark Age, just as Hitler plunged Germany back into a (largely imaginary) ancient mindset with pseudo scientific concepts of race replacing the older tribal categories. Both were "revolutionary" leaders of a peculiar modern sort: contemporary political techniques merged with archaic ideas. Even before the fall of the Shah, I wrote that Khomeini was the latest example of a well-established concept: clerical fascism.

To those who argue that the flight from freedom is limited to one group or another, of one area or another, or one religion or another, I can only recommend remedial reading of contemporary history. And to those who say we should just abandon the peoples of the Middle East to their own misery and oppression, I can only say that there is no escape for us from the evil of Islamic fascism. It is not just an academic question; tyrants hate America, and will invariably try to kill or dominate us. We need to shed all illusions about the nature of such regimes, above all the mirage that they are, after all, "just like us," and whatever differences we have can be resolved by patient negotiation, or cultural exchange, or simple deterrence. I don't believe any of that. I think they are implacable enemies of all free societies. I think the very nature of those regimes compels them to attack us in every possible way, as they have. I think they have waged war against us for a long time (the terror war was clearly in full swing by the late seventies, and probably started back in the late sixties), and will continue to do it until they either win or lose. The policy question, on which our own survival may well depend, is how best to defeat them.

Modern revolutionary regimes like the Islamic Republic have fallen both because their own people turned against them, and because they were defeated on the battlefield. In each case, the revolutionary ideology was discredited. We humiliated the fascist revolution in the Second World War, and fascism was drained of its mass appeal. We do not know how European fascism would have ended (or even if it would have ended) if the Axis had won the war, but China today probably represents the first case of a mature fascist regime, one in which the ideology is now bloodless, but whose regime remains very nasty, corrupt, and potentially aggressive. Communism had lost much of its appeal in other Warsaw Pact countries even before we defeated the Soviet Empire. Years before the wall was breeched, very few people wanted their country to become a new Bulgaria, and Pope John Paul II once wryly forecast that the last communist on earth would be a North American nun.

Islamic fascism may yet do us in, but it may also be on the same track to the losers' circle that the fascists and communists raced down. Machiavelli reminds us that tyranny is the least stable form of government, and the Islamic Republic is extremely brittle. The Iranian people loathe it, and would gladly trade it for the Westminster model or their own fine 1906 Constitution. Messianic movements of the sort led by the Islamic Republic can inspire masses of people, but they are uniquely vulnerable, because any dramatic setback raises a frightening question: has divine support suddenly been removed? Setbacks to the mullahs' grand design to dominate the world can have devastating effects on the regime in Tehran, and the battlefields of Iraq, Israel, and Lebanon are in constant flux. It is impossible to predict the outcomes, even in the most important theater of all, Iraq.

Most Iraqis, even though they are still voting along "religious" lines, have shown little affection for a new caliphate or Islamic republic. No sooner had they voted for the religious blocs than they sat down and renegotiated the division of power. It's not textbook post-electoral politics, but it bespeaks a distinctly nonfanatical approach to government. Several recent polls show that al Qaeda's popularity ratings are careening downward, while our own are rising. I think these positive symptoms are the result of three main factors: the failure of the terrorists to drive us out of the Middle East, the recognition by most people that the terrorists, from al Qaeda to Hezbollah (that is, from Sunni to Shi'ite), are evil and must be defeated, and the near-universal conviction that the Islamic Republic of Iran is not the sort of place where one wants to live. That mullahcracy is the closest thing on earth to the much-ballyhooed "caliphate" so dear to the mouths of the jihadis, and most Iraqis, as most Middle Easterners, think it stinks.

There are some hopeful signs in Iraq, beginning with the anti-al Qaeda campaign in Anbar Province waged by Sunni sheikhs in concert with Coalition forces, including Iraqi Shi'ite soldiers. That is a real blow to the mullahs, as is the encouraging campaign against Iranian-supported terrorist cells in other areas of Iraq. From the Iranian point of view, the most frightening aspect of these developments is the change in the mindset of many Iraqis. These events suggest that many Iraqis have changed their bet on the outcome of the war; they no longer believe that the terrorists will surely win, and they are helping us defeat them. We could not be so effective without the active support of large numbers of Iraqis who give us information, gossip and tips, and even fight back against the terrorists. If that spreads, the mullahs can lose the grip they believe they have over millions of Iraqis.

Finally, there is the desire for freedom. The "realists" to the contrary notwithstanding, most all of us yearn for both freedom and security, and there is no doubt that the exercise of freedom is difficult. That's why Ben Franklin warned that while we had created a republic, we would have to fight to preserve it. The demons that Erich

Fromm described so well do torture our souls, and even though there are enormous variations from one culture to another, no society is exempt either from a yearning to be free, or from the totalitarian temptation. Both the desire for freedom and the fear of freedom are universal, and most human beings will fight for freedom when the circumstances are right.

That's the nub of the question: timing. The time is not always right, and history is full of examples of romantic democrats losing everything by fighting desperately when they had no real chance of success. I believe that today the time *is* right. Ours is a moment characterized by radical change, when tyrants feel threatened, when freedom is advancing, and revolution is the defining characteristic of international affairs. John Paul II, Ronald Reagan, Margaret Thatcher, Lech Walesa, and the others all understood that, which is why Reagan was able to announce that the evil empire's days were numbered, and why John Paul II told his followers "be not afraid."

The call for democratic revolution is not at all naive; actually it's far more realistic than the self-defeating inaction of the "realists." If we had supported the revolutionaries with the enthusiasm they deserve, I have little doubt we would not be engaged in Kabuki dances around the mullahs. Nor would we be limited to such unpalatable alternatives as appeasement-masquerading-as-diplomacy with the

UN and the IAEA on the one hand, and a potentially disastrous bombing campaign on the other.

Revolution is our most lethal weapon against the mullahs. We should have used it years ago, and must use it now.

ACKNOWLEDGMENTS

The Iranian Time Bomb is the brainchild of Truman "Mac" Talley of St. Martin's Press, my longtime editor there. He's been a wonderful editor, I sometimes fear one of the last of a vanishing breed of editors who work hard with their authors and then really edit. So primary thanks go to him.

Equal credit goes, as usual, to Lynn Chu and Glen Hartley, the outstanding literary agents at Writers' Representatives, Inc.

For the last twenty years I've had the singular blessing of being permitted to work at the American Enterprise Institute in Washington, where I can find out most anything I need to know by walking down the hall and asking some brilliant and collegial person. Thanks to my colleagues, and to AEI's president, Chris DeMuth, and vice president, David Gerson, who have always supported my work and still do.

I am told that writing books comes easily to some authors; it certainly does not for me. Somehow Barbara Ledeen tolerates my bad temper and enriches a love that is well along in its fourth decade. Such a woman!

This book was written quickly, and required considerable scholarly legwork, which was provided with good humor and great efficiency by Golnar Oveyssi and Daniel Holman at AEI. They even caught some of my mistakes along the way, although some no doubt remain.

My recent work on terrorism and Iran is driven in no small part by our children's direct involvement in the war. Simone has served in both Iraq and Afghanistan, and Gabriel is preparing for his second deployment to Iraq with his marines. Daniel has already committed to several years in a marine uniform after he completes his undergraduate work. Many of our friends' children are similarly engaged, and we are all inspired by them. They, and indeed every military person I know who has been in theater, knows that Iran is the major enemy. Would that the politicians and intellectuals had a similar grasp of our current condition.

INDEX